# THE GOSPEL OF GRACE

# THE GOSPEL OF GRACE

The Way of Salvation in the Wesleyan Tradition

## Kenneth Cain Kinghorn

### CHARLES R. BROCKWELL, Jr.
*GENERAL EDITOR*

ABINGDON PRESS / Nashville

THE GOSPEL OF GRACE:
THE WAY OF SALVATION IN THE WESLEYAN TRADITION

**Library of Congress Cataloging-in-Publication Data**

Kinghorn, Kenneth C.
   The gospel of Grace : the way of salvation in the Wesleyan tradition / Kenneth Cain Kinghorn.
      p. cm.—(Teachings of United Methodism)
   Includes bibliographical references and index.
   ISBN 0-687-15654-8 (alk. paper)
   1. Grace (Theology) 2. Creation. 3. Sin. 4. Conversion
5. Sanctification. 6. United Methodist Church (U.S.)—Doctrines.
7. Methodist Church—Doctrines. I. Title. II. Series.
BT761.2.K46   1992
234—dc20                                          91-32844
                                                        CIP

MANUFACTURED IN THE UNITED STATES OF AMERICA

*To*

*John Montgomery*

# CONTENTS

# CONTENTS

# FOREWORD

*B*efore and during the 1988 General Conference of The United Methodist Church discussion centered around a new theological statement. That statement calls us to reaffirm and redefine our standards of doctrine. It also calls us "to reclaim and renew the distinctive United Methodist doctrinal heritage . . . for the life and mission of the whole Church today." All of us are to share in that task.

Kenneth Kinghorn contributes to this discussion in this volume. The theme of this book is that God as loving parent reaches out through grace to bring each person into a growing personal relationship with God. The theme is sounded in the first chapter on "Creation" and carried through the succeeding chapters.

This is a timely book. There is renewed interest among United Methodists on doctrinal matters. In addition, we have difficulty accepting God's grace. A recent study concluded that 68 percent of United Methodist adults find it difficult to accept salvation as God's gift.

Kinghorn's warm-hearted treatment of grace is soundly based in Scripture. His illustrations range from the oft-repeated children's prayer, "God is great and God is good" to reference to *The Book of Discipline*, hymns, John Wesley, and other eminent theologians.

The annotated bibliography is one of the valuable resources of this book. Some fifty works are listed, to which the serious student may refer for further study. Hundreds of Scripture citations are arranged by the chapter titles. A listing of hymns and other resources are also valuable references.

My hope is that this book will be widely used by pastors and local church members in discussions about their own spiritual life and relationships with God. It may truly be a means of God's grace for those of us who are disciples in the last part of the twentieth century.

Bishop R. Sheldon Duecker

# PREFACE

*B*ishop R. Sheldon Duecker asserts, "United Methodists don't have a *common* understanding of basic Christian beliefs." He reports a layperson saying to him, "I hunger for a clear sense of my United Methodist *identity.*"

What is United Methodist doctrine? Many voices respond to this question, ranging from those hoping to instruct the Church to caucuses intending to pressure it.

None of these voices, however, speaks for the Church. "No person, no paper, no organization, has the authority to speak officially for The United Methodist Church, this right having been reserved exclusively to the General Conference under the Constitution" *(Discipline,* par. 610.1).

This book is the first of a series called "We Believe." This is a series of books written for United Methodist laypersons to advance self-understanding and identity by communicating United Methodist doctrine directly from General Conference approved documents. The books in this series are *How Do United Methodists Do Theology?; Who Is the God We Worship?; What Is the Church?; The Gospel of Grace; Methodism: Practicing the Love of God;* and *United Methodist Ministry and Mission.*

The authors have set forth what the Church officially teaches rather than what each thinks the Church ought to teach. They focus on the question: "What theological teaching has The United Methodist Church 'owned' through its established conciliar processes of decision making and teaching?"

Thus these books are not personal statements or caucus declarations. They present the teachings of John Wesley; *The Book of Discipline;* and other official United Methodist documents (e.g., *The Book of Resolutions; The United Methodist Hymnal, The Book of Services*).

The authors in this series do not proceed by lining up the categories of systematic theology and saying what the Church teaches under each heading. They pursue core elements of "substantial, experimental, practical divinity" through the Church's own documents. This method of beginning with how doctrine affects Christian life is characteristically Wesleyan.

John Wesley used our doctrines to specify the scriptural, historic Christian teachings that were the particular emphases of "the work of God called Methodism." Primarily, these were teachings relating to divine-human interaction and to sanctification. The books in this series remind us of this heritage and include United Methodist, not just Wesleyan, doctrine.

What might these books do for The United Methodist Church? (1) They will bring before the Church its common body of official doctrinal sources and survey what these sources teach. (2) They will demonstrate how the Church's workbooks and worship books are doctrinal documents. (3) This will advance the teaching office of the General Conference. (4) They will point out where the Church's doctrine needs clarification and better organization for consistency and coherence. (5) They will promote discussion of whether the Church needs a theological secretariat to assist our highest governing council in defining United Methodist doctrine.

The United Methodist Church is part of the community of Wesleyan denominations, but The United Methodist Church has larger responsibilities. One of these is the formal development of doctrine. The books in this series contribute to the maturing of that ministry among and for "the people called United Methodists."

Charles W. Brockwell, Jr.
General Editor

# INTRODUCTION

*P*erhaps no single word better sums up the message of the Bible than *grace*. The biblical subject of grace permeates all aspects of Christian theology, and we comprehend Christianity only as we understand grace. This rich theme opens the doors into many theological doctrines and unlocks their essential truths. Grace pertains to the doctrines of God, creation, providence, the sacraments, the atonement, Christian vocation, Old Testament history, the New Testament church, prayer, spiritual gifts, and liturgy— too many subjects to consider in a volume of this length. This book focuses on *Christian experience*, which in Wesleyan theology constitutes the most important aspect of biblical religion. These pages explain what John Wesley called "practical divinity." By the term *practical divinity* we mean "the experiential realization of the gospel of Jesus Christ" (*Discipline*, 50).

In accord with the general plan for this series of books on Wesleyan beliefs, *The Gospel of Grace* builds on United Methodism's recognized doctrinal standards. The primary and ultimate source of authority for the Church is, of course, the Bible. The United Methodist *Book of Discipline* states, "The basic measure of authenticity in doctrinal standards, whether formally established or received by tradition, has been their fidelity to the apostolic faith grounded in Scripture and evidenced in the life of the Church through the centuries" (*Discipline*, 42).

United Methodism also recognizes other sources of authority certified by the General Conferences of the church. These official Church guidelines include the denomination's *Book of Discipline, The United Methodist Hymnal, The Book of Worship for Church and Home*, sections from *The Discipline of the Evangelical United Brethren, The Book of Services, The Book of Resolutions, The COCU* (Churches of Christ Uniting) *Consensus, Guidelines: The United Methodist Church and the Charismatic Movement*, and certain other papers and reports adopted by United Methodism's General Conference. In addition, from its beginning, The Methodist Episcopal Church has viewed as models of doctrinal exposition John Wesley's *Standard Sermons* and his *Explanatory Notes upon the New Testament*. It is important to note that Wesleyan hymnody has served in practice as the most important single means of communicating and preserving the doctrinal substance of the gospel (see *Discipline*, 55).

At a secondary level, this book cites a number of semiofficial documents of the Church. While these sources do not stand as binding authorities on doctrinal matters, they do have an *ex officio* status within United Methodism. This body of material consists of such recognized standard works as *The Journal of John Wesley; The Letters of John Wesley;* John Fletcher's *Checks Against Antinomianism;* Philip William Otterbein's sermons and letters; Adam Clarke's *Commentaries;* Richard Watson's *Theological Institutes; The Cyclopaedia of Methodism*, edited by Matthew Simpson; *The History of American Methodism*, 3 volumes, edited by Emory S. Bucke; and *The Encyclopedia of World Methodism*, 2 volumes, edited by Nolan B. Harmon. Again, these works do not constitute official doctrinal authorities in The United Methodist Church. They do, however, give us insight into the mainstream thought and life of the Wesleyan tradition.

Then, at a third level, certain other books commend themselves as useful reference materials for this study of the Wesleyan understanding of grace. Although these writings do not have even semiofficial authority in the Church, they do enjoy wide recognition as being substantially faithful to the Wesleyan tradition. With frequency, references to these works appear in monographs and articles about Wesleyan thought and life. To the extent that these books contain nothing "contrary to the present existing and established standards of doctrine" (First Restrictive Rule, *Discipline*, 25), and as they serve the church, we turn to them in this present volume. A sampling of books in this category include such recognized works as Ole E. Borgen's *John Wesley on the Sacraments*; William R. Cannon's *The Theology of John Wesley*; Robert E. Chiles's *Theological Transition in American Methodism*; Albert C. Outler's *Evangelism in the Wesleyan Spirit*; John L. Peters's *Christian Perfection and American Methodism*; William E. Sangster's *The Path to Perfection*; Philip S. Watson's *The Message of the Wesleys*; and Colin W. Williams's *John Wesley's Theology Today*. I have cited a number of such books, along with some recent titles, with the belief that they contribute to our understanding of the gospel of grace.

At the beginning of the twentieth century the growth of secular intellectual currents and the waning of doctrinal discipline led to a decline of interest in Methodism's theological heritage. The denomination experienced "a steady dilution of the force of the Articles of Religion as the Church's constitutional standards of doctrine" (*Discipline*, 55). In many circles the emphasis shifted from "who we are" to "what we do." Action seemed more important than faith. By no means was this neglect of the Wesleyan tradition universal among the people called Methodists. Studies in Wesleyan theology and concern for Christian experience have continued, even if these interests have not dominated the agenda of the Church. Now, the situation seems to be changing. Breezes of theological and spiritual renewal are stirring.

Out of this context a revived interest in the Wesleyan tradition has surfaced. United Methodism's 1988 *Book of Discipline* voiced a fresh appreciation for the value of the Church's Wesleyan heritage. The 1988 General Conference of United Methodism agreed:

> In recent decades there has been a strong recovery of interest in Wesley and in the more classic traditions of Christian thought. This recovery has been part of a broad resurgence of Reformation theology and practice in Europe and America, renewing the historical legacy of Protestantism in the context of the modern world. These trends have been reinforced in North America by the reaffirmation of evangelical piety. (*Discipline*, 56)

The 1988 General Conference of The United Methodist Church concurred that, "the heart of our task is to reclaim and renew the distinctive United Methodist doctrinal heritage, which rightly belongs to our common heritage as Christians, for the life and mission of the whole Church today" (*Discipline*, 56).

Our present subject—the doctrine of grace—stands at the heart of the gospel itself. The *Book of Discipline* articulates the belief that

> Grace pervades our understanding of Christian faith and life. By grace we mean the undeserved, unmerited, and loving action of God in human existence through the

ever-present Holy Spirit. While the grace of God is undivided, it precedes salvation as "prevenient grace," continues in "justifying grace," and is brought to fruition in "sanctifying grace." . . . The restoration of God's image in our lives requires divine grace to renew our fallen nature (*Discipline*, 45-46).

The first of John Wesley's *Standard Sermons*, "Salvation by Faith," deals with the subject of grace. Wesley opened that collection of sermons with the following thesis:

All the blessings which God hath bestowed upon [us] are of His mere grace, bounty, or favour; His free, undeserved favour; favour altogether undeserved; [we] having no claim to the least of His mercies. It was free grace that 'formed [us] of the dust of the ground, and breathed into [us] a living soul,' and stamped on that soul the image of God, and 'put all things under [our] feet' (SSS, I, 37).

So this is a book about the gospel of grace, with specific reference to Scripture and to the Wesleyan heritage.

Quotations in this book retain original spellings and wordings, unless otherwise specified. To save space, I have employed an abbreviation for each reference cited; this code appears alphabetically in the appendix to the book "Annotated Bibliography and Keys to Citations and References," pages 121-129. Also, this book contains indexes of hymns, references to the United Methodist *Book of Discipline*, a key Scripture index, and an index of subjects and persons. Unless indicated, the Scripture quotations in this book are taken from the New Revised Standard Version of the Bible.

I wish to thank Lydia Hoyle and the group of lay Christians of First United Methodist Church, Lexington, Kentucky, who read this book in its manuscript form and offered comments. I wish also to thank Charles Brockwell for conceiving the idea for this series of books on the doctrine and mission of The United Methodist Church. My faculty colleagues of Asbury Theological Seminary enrich my thinking with their knowledge, wisdom, humor, and spiritual vitality. And, as always, the competent folks at Abingdon Press make working on a book project a pleasure.

Kenneth Cain Kinghorn
Pentecost 1991

# Chapter I

# CREATION

*The great Creator from his work return'd*
*Magnificent, his six days' work, a world.*
—John Milton (1608–1674)

*T*o ponder the vastness of the creation and the infinity of time constitutes one of the most awe-producing experiences possible for a human being. In the face of the greatness of the created order, reason collapses and varieties of emotions sweep over us. Since humankind began to exist on this planet, these feelings alternate between wonder at the immensity and beauty of the world, anxiety concerning our significance in the vast cosmos, concern about our future beyond this life, and frustration over our inability either to fathom or to control nature's power.

The psalmist David expressed this common sense of awe.

> When I look at your heavens,
> the work of your fingers,
> the moon and the stars that
> you have established;
> what are human beings that you
> are mindful of them,
> mortals that you care for
> them? (Ps. 8:3-4)

From a biblical point of view we can no more separate creation from God than we can dissociate a symphony from its composer or a poem from its author. The doctrine of creation lies at the foundation of all Christian theology: the Creator created creation. Our view of creation touches on such important issues as how we perceive God, ourselves, our neighbors, and the world. The biblical doctrine of creation sets the stage for understanding history and provides us with the context for comprehending God's purposes for us in this life.

The Bible opens with the fundamental affirmation, "In the beginning . . . God created the heavens and the earth . . . " (Gen. 1:1). The church through history has echoed the conviction of the biblical writers that God made everything that exists and that God stands absolutely sovereign over creation, providence, and redemption. So The United Methodist Church joins with other Christian churches in confessing the ancient ecumenical statement, "I believe in God, the Father Almighty, creator of heaven and earth" (The Apostles' Creed, Ecumenical Version; see *UMH*, 882).

The created order is not autonomous or self-sufficient. It belongs to God and ever remains dependent upon God (Exod. 19:5; Lev. 25:23; Pss. 24:1; 50:10). The creation, therefore, is not free to go its independent way apart from its designer and maker. The Christian doctrine of creation points to the truth that the creation is not accidental. God created with purpose. Paul affirms, "In him all things in heaven and on earth were created, things visible and invisible, whether thrones or dominions or rulers or powers—all things have been created through him and for him. He himself is before all things, and in him all things hold together" (Col. 1:16-17; see also Rev. 4:11). And at the center of God's concern is humankind, made in God's image.

The Christian doctrine of creation is so astonishingly wonderful that theology quickly becomes doxology, a wish to praise the Lord for mighty works (e.g., Ps. 148). In an expansive expression of thanksgiving and praise for the creation, the psalmist David declared,

> The earth is the LORD's and all
> that is in it,
> the world, and those who live
> in it;
> for he has founded it. (Ps. 24:1-2)

Through the great hymns of the church, United Methodists join with Christians of other church bodies in singing about the wonder and glory of God's creation:

> I sing the almighty power of God,
> That made the mountains rise,
> That spread the flowing seas abroad,
> And built the lofty skies.
> I sing the wisdom that ordained
> The sun to rule the day;
> The moon shines full at God's command,
> And all the stars obey.
> (Isaac Watts; see *UMH*, 152)

Truly, "The heavens are telling the glory of God;/ and the firmament proclaims his handiwork" (Ps. 19:1). A well-known children's prayer underscores the most basic theological theme in Scripture—*God is great; God is good.* All Christian doctrine rests on the belief that God is the infinite creator and we are the finite created ones. "In him we live and move and have our being" (Acts 17:28).

## 1. THE BIBLICAL DOCTRINE OF CREATION

The biblical doctrine of creation stands out as unique among all the religious and philosophical theories of the earth's beginnings and humankind's place in the world.

History has produced numerous speculative notions about creation.

*Dualism* posits the view that the world is the product of the struggle between two co-eternal beings—one good and one evil.

*Platonism* teaches that God was limited in the creation because God formed the universe from preexisting matter.

*Materialism* holds the view that the universe came into being as a consequence of the accidental mutations of energy and matter, apart from the activity of God.

*Pantheism* contends that the universe emanates from God and that God is one with, and inseparable from, the world.

The Bible offers an understanding of the universe that stands apart from the numerous hypothetical philosophies about the origin and meaning of the world.

*(a) God is the source of all that exists.* The scriptures teach us that the one true God is the sole author of creation, and this biblical doctrine contrasts dramatically with the numerous cosmologies of the ancient Near East that were contemporary with the Old Testament writers. The ancient Babylonian creation epic theorized that the universe emerged as a product of hostilities between different gods. That document tells that Marduk, a god of Babylon, seized preexisting matter from a competing god. Allegedly, Marduk fashioned the material world in such a way as to contaminate it with evil. The Bible, however, gives us an entirely different account of creation. Scripture attributes the origin of the universe to one God who created all things *ex nihilo* (out of nothing).

Another creation legend contends that matter has existed from eternity. According to this theory, matter has no beginning; it stands co-eternal with God. Therefore, when God created the world he was restricted to the materials that were on hand. Allegedly, God did not create matter, but rearranged existing materials. Again, the Bible presents quite a different view of creation. According to Scripture, matter had no existence before God created it. The universe came into being only as God willed it; the world is not self-eternal or self-originated. The psalmist declared,

> Before the mountains were
> brought forth,
> or ever you had formed the
> earth and the world,
> from everlasting to everlasting
> you are God. (Ps. 90:2)

Scripture reiterates again and again the affirmation that God created the universe out of nothing (Gen. 1:1; Job 38:4-13; Ps. 102:25; John 1:3; Acts 14:15; Heb. 11:3).

In the mid-nineteenth century, another theory of the earth's origins emerged—a philosophy of materialism. This theory hypothesized that, over billions of years, the world and its inhabitants developed by chance. According to the philosophy of materialism, matter spontaneously sprang from nothing—perhaps as the result of an accidental cosmic explosion—without the activity of a divine creator. Advocates of this view speculate that inert matter slowly evolved into organic life; and, in time, there appeared lower forms of life, such as fish and worms. Gradually these species further transmuted into primates, and eventually into human life. At the heart of this hypothesis is the doctrine that "natural selection," although without purpose, randomly produced the world we know without the intervention of God the Creator.

In contrast to this speculative philosophical theory, the Christian doctrine of creation affirms that the universe exists solely because the sovereign Creator wills that it should exist (Gen. 1:1-31; Neh. 9:6; Ps. 33:6; Rev. 4:11). Scripture reiterates the important truth that God absolutely determines all things, and God stands over all his works. God's world is not accidental, haphazard, or aimless. "All things came into being through him, and without him not one thing came into being" (John 1:3). If God removed his hand, the universe would collapse.

Numerous biblical references tell that each of the members of the Trinity was involved in the creation. When the Scriptures speak of God as creator, they refer to the Godhead—Father, Son, and Holy Spirit (Gen. 1:2; Job 26:13; 33:4; Ps. 104:30; John 1:1-3; I Cor. 8:6; Col. 1:16-17). The creation is the product of an all-wise, all-powerful, and all-loving God who made the world for God's purposes.

*(b) Scripture distinguishes between the Creator and the creation.* God stands above creation, and we must not merge the Creator with the created. As wonderful as humankind is, there remains what Søren Kierkegaard has called "an infinite qualitative distinction" between God and us. One aspect of the church's worship is the recognition that, although we stand out as the highest of God's creation, we are not gods or manifestations of God's being. God alone is divine and infinite. The following hymn expresses this truth.

> Immortal, invisible, God only wise,
> In light inaccessible hid from our eyes,
> Most blessed, most glorious, the Ancient of Days,
> Almighty, victorious, thy great name we praise.
> (Walter Chalmers Smith; see *UMH*, 103)

We must never confuse the created with the Creator. God is infinite and sovereign; we are finite and dependent.

Biblical cosmology differs sharply from those religious

systems that imagine the creation emanates from God, as rays stream from the sun. This ancient cosmology is called *pantheism,* and this theory circulates yet today. Pantheism holds that God permeates everything and, consequently, we cannot separate the creator from those things he creates. According to this theory, God and the universe are fused into one—the world is a part of God, and God is a part of the world. Pantheistic thought believes that the way of salvation consists of probing deep within ourselves to find the part of God that resides within us. Allegedly, we discover that we are mini-gods by introspectively penetrating the depth of our own being. We see expressions of this pantheistic thinking in Hinduism, in nineteenth-century transcendentalism, and in the so-called New Age theologies.

In making the point that God exists as distinct from the world he made, the biblical writers speak of God as a heavenly Father. When the biblical writers refer to God as "he," the intent is not to focus on God's gender, but rather to stress that God is *personal* and *distinct.* By use of the personal pronoun, Scripture makes clear that God is not an "it" or a nonpersonal force. Jesus taught us to pray to God not as a mere concept or idea, but as our heavenly Parent—"Our Father in heaven, hallowed be your name . . . " (Matt. 6:9). Paul never tired of speaking of God as a personal and loving father (Rom. 8:15-17; Gal. 4:6, 7). The Christian teaching that God is our heavenly Father stands out as an unparalleled doctrine among the religions of the world. In 1988 the General Conference of the Church affirmed the use of this biblical language and imagery in all its forms in the Church's hymns, liturgy, teaching, and in all areas of our common life together (BOR, 596).

The Bible strictly forbids the veneration of any thing or person other than the God of Scripture (Exod. 20:4;

Lev. 26:1; Deut. 7:25; 11:16; Isa. 42:8; I John 5:21). Both nature's wonder and human glory are derived and reflected, not self-generated. No created thing possesses intrinsic divinity within itself—God alone deserves our worship. John Wesley pointed out the distinction between us and our maker: "Man is a merely dependent being. . . . Dependence is woven into his very nature; so that, should God withdraw from him, he would sink into nothing" (WJWJ, IX, 456). Failure to worship and serve God constitutes the first and greatest sin (Exod. 20:1-6).

Although God stands above all creation, God wishes to reveal himself to humankind. God does not hide from us, although we may hide from God (Gen. 3:8). As our Father in heaven, God desires that we know him, and God longs for us to respond to his loving initiative. The gospel of grace flows from the biblical teaching that God is a divine personality who wishes to enter into a personal relationship with each of us as our heavenly Father (Deut. 32:6; Ps. 68:5; Isa. 64:8; Mal. 2:10; Matt. 7:11; 23:9; I Cor. 8:6; Eph. 4:6; Heb. 12:9).

*(c) The goodness of creation.* The ancient Eastern religious doctrine of dualism holds that two opposing divine powers have existed from eternity. The good power is absolute spirit, untainted by matter. The malevolent power created the material world, which dualism regards as evil. Dualism contends that our spirits are imprisoned in our bodies and that we find salvation by retreating from the material world to meditate on the realm of the spirit, which alone is pure and good. Some dualists go so far as to deprive or punish their bodies to show their contempt for material things. Still others seek "out-of-body experiences" where they can presumably enter into an awareness of spirits or "ascended masters" who are free from the restricting confinement of

corporeal existence. A few dualists live licentiously, reasoning that the material body is of little consequence. In contrast to counting matter as evil, the biblical view of creation holds that God made nothing that is evil. Genesis tells us that God pronounced the material world "very good" (Gen. 1:31). We, too, should value the creation and serve as earth's trustees, under a divine mandate to assume responsibility for it as faithful stewards. William Temple (*Nature, Man, and God* [New York: Macmillan, 1949], 478) correctly stated, "Christianity is the most avowedly materialist of all the great religions." God gave us this physical world as a wonderful gift to use and enjoy. Christian theology does not despise the world God has made.

Evil arises not out of material things, but out of the perversion of the good that God created. Sin lies not in our contact with the world, but results from the misuse of what God created for our good. To attempt to satisfy our needs and desires in the wrong way or at the wrong time leads us to pervert and to distort God's created order. The story of Adam and Eve illustrates these truths. In a letter to his wife, General Robert E. Lee wrote, "What a glorious world Almighty God has given us! How thankless and ungrateful we are, and how we labor to mar His gifts."

## 2. HUMANKIND IN THE IMAGE OF GOD

The highest of God's creative acts was his creation of the man and the woman in his own image (Gen. 1:27). Theologians have pondered at length the *imago dei* (image of God) in humankind. Details in theological discussions about the *imago dei* differ mostly because authors stress different aspects of this important theological subject. Almost all theologians agree on certain fundamental points related to our having been created in the image of God. And the reality of this unique status of human beings excites us with far-reaching implications.

*(a) God created human beings as unique in the world.* Humankind is of a different order than the angels, the animals, the plants, and inanimate things (Ps. 8:5-8). Human beings have more than physical bodies—we also possess *spirits* (Job 32:8; Prov. 20:27). In contrast to his creation of all else, we are singularly endowed by God with the ability to reason. We have self-consciousness; we can make rational judgments; we possess memory and imagination. We experience the emotions of sorrow, fear, desire, hope, joy, and love. With proper instruction, humankind can distinguish between true and false, good and bad, appropriate and inappropriate. In contrast to the rest of creation, human beings can invent machines, compose music, write poetry, paint pictures, think abstractly, dream dreams, and see visions. Truly, created in the image of God, we are "fearfully and wonderfully made" (Ps. 139:14).

God's first and most profound commandment to the man and the woman was, "Be fruitful and multiply, and fill the earth" (Gen. 1:28). The supreme human creative capacity consists of the ability to procreate another human being. All of our other abilities—such as developing nuclear power, inventing technology, and building great cities—cannot compare with the awesome human potential to produce and nurture children in the training and instruction of the Lord (Deut. 4:9; 6:7; Prov. 22:6; Matt. 16:26; Eph. 6:4; Tit. 2:4). God's greatest gift to us is a *child* (Matt. 19:14). Any activity aimed at the deliberate destruction of a developing human life constitutes the gravest of sins (Gen. 9:6; Exod. 20:13). Jesus underscored the sanctity of human life by forbidding us even to call another person "a fool"

(Matt. 5:22; see also I John 3:15). To do so is to deny another his or her status as created in God's image. Distinct from the animal kingdom, humankind possesses a special dignity because God created us in his own likeness, and we can fellowship with him in this life and in eternity.

Of course, human beings have some things in common with the material world—our bodies are made of the dust of the earth (Gen. 2:7; 3:19; Ps. 103:14). We also have some things in common with God—we are made in God's likeness (Gen. 1:26-27; James 3:9). The 1980 General Conference of The United Methodist Church passed a resolution that contains the following conviction:

> Humankind enjoys a unique place in God's universe. On the one hand we are simply one of God's many finite creatures, made from the "dust of the earth," bounded in time and space, fallible in judgment, limited in control, dependent upon our Creator, and interdependent with all other creatures. On the other hand we are created in the very image of God, with the divine spirit breathed into us, and entrusted with "dominion" over God's creation. . . . We are simultaneously co-creatures with all creation, and, because of the divine summons, co-creators with God of the world in which we live. (BOR 1988, 43)

God created us less than God, but above the natural order (Ps. 8:4-9). We are not one with nature, although we participate in nature.

In addition to setting humankind above all the rest of the creation, God made each individual a special person. God calls every person by name, even when he or she is yet in the mother's womb (Ps. 139:13-16; see also Luke 1:44). Uniquely, human beings possess the capacity for spiritual fellowship with God (see WJWJ, VI, 244). God invested humankind alone with moral responsibility and ethical accountability. After the creation of the man and the woman, the Lord addressed them as "you"—a term never used for the animals (Gen. 3:9). William Gladstone said, "Man is the crown of the visible creation, and studies upon man . . . conversant with his nature, his works, his duties, and his destinies are the highest of all studies" (*Midlothian Speeches, 1879* [New York: Humanities Press, 1971], 249).

(b) *God endowed human beings with the qualities of dependence and independence.* Wesleyan theology seeks to keep in balance two aspects of our humanity: We are dependent, and we are independent; restricted and yet free. On the one hand, we are mortal beings who rely entirely upon God for life and preservation (Ps. 49:12). As Paul contended, "[God] gives to all mortals life and breath and all things" (Acts 17:25; see also Neh. 9:6). We have no existence or ability apart from the creating and sustaining grace of the sovereign God. And we can do nothing without God's permission and enabling.

On the other hand, God endowed us with a relative degree of freedom and independence, especially in moral decisions and spiritual relationships (Exod. 32:26; Deut. 30:19; Josh. 24:15; I Kings 18:21). Within certain perimeters, we can select our priorities, make decisions, and spend time and energy as we please. To a limited extent, we possess free will and the capacity for self-determination. We are not bound by the external environment; we can choose the moral directions we take. Commenting on the creation story in Genesis, biblical scholar Walter Brueggemann rightly observes, "The grace of God is that the creature whom he has *caused* to be, he now *lets* be" (*Genesis* [Atlanta: John Knox Press, 1982], 28).

Those who focus too much on our dependence reduce

us to robots that move only at the direction of forces outside ourselves. Since the time of John Locke and David Hume some philosophers have insisted that a human being is but a *tabula rasa* (a blank tablet) who has no freedom to act or think independently of external forces and environment. This school of thought reduces humankind to a neurological machine that predictably responds to stimuli. Then, within Christian theology, one stream of thought surmises that our creaturely status renders us so helplessly dependent that our salvation hinges entirely upon the operation of divine election. The doctrine of predestination means that God chooses who will be saved or lost and causes his desired purposes to happen.

In reaction to all forms of determinism, some so strongly emphasize human ability and free choice that they insist that persons are free to choose or do anything they will—even to the point of achieving merit before God. This way of thinking can slip into the ancient error of *Pelagianism,* which boasts that we possess the natural ability to take initial steps toward salvation, apart from God's grace. Those who focus too much on human freedom and ability tend to forget that salvation comes by grace alone (Acts 15:11; Rom. 3:24; 5:15; 11:6; Eph. 2:8-9; Tit. 2:11; 3:7). This brand of theology sees good works as meritorious before God—a serious theological error. The truth lies in balancing our creatureliness and dependence on grace with our capacity to make moral choices and, with God's assistance, to perform responsible good works.

Tragically, sin has darkened our spiritual sensibilities and clouded our minds. We are capable of every kind of self-deception (Jer. 17:9; Rom. 3:13). The English cardinal John Henry Newman, in *The Dream of Geronitus,* described humankind this way:

O man, strange composite of Heaven and earth!
Majesty dwarf'd to baseness! fragrant flower
Running to poisonous seed! and seeming worth
Cloaking corruption! weakness mastering power!

Wesleyan theology holds that the image of God within us has been tragically marred, but not entirely erased. Through grace we can know God and experience the integration of our minds and spirits.

*(c) God commissioned human beings as his supreme agents in the world.* God positioned the man and the woman over all the rest of creation. The writer of Genesis states:

Then God said, "Let us make humankind in our image, according to our likeness; and let them have dominion over the fish of the sea, and over the birds of the air, and over the cattle, and over all the wild animals of the earth, and over every creeping thing that creeps upon the earth."
So God created humankind in his image,
in the image of God he created them;
male and female he created them.
(Gen. 1:26-27; see also Heb. 2:8; James 3:7)

We humans have the responsibility under God to stand above everything God has made. The psalmist wrote:

You have made them a little
lower than God,
and crowned them with glory
and honor.
You have given them dominion
over the works of your hands;
you have put all things under
their feet.
(Ps. 8:5-6; see also Gen. 9:2; Matt. 6:26; 12:12)

God, of course, has supreme and ultimate dominion over the earth. Yet, God intended that we exercise a delegated authority over the created order and serve as his representatives in the world.

The history of humanity reveals that humankind has demonstrated a persistent tendency to worship nature or some aspect of the material world. God designated us as nature's masters, not nature's servants. Our destiny does not lie in some force within the created order, such as the sun or the Nile River. Belief in astrology—the theory that the stars influence our lives—is pagan and far from the biblical understanding of creation. The practice of venerating the creation is a betrayal of the dignity of our nature and the purpose of our calling. Only God controls the universe and God alone deserves our worship. Dietrich Bonhoeffer reminds us, "We do not rule because we do not know the world as God's creation, and because we do not receive our dominion as God-given but grasp it for ourselves" (*Creation and Fall: A Theological Interpretation of Genesis 1–3* [New York: Macmillan, 1959], 38). God does not intend for us to be subservient or subordinate to nature; God commissioned us to rule over it.

Our position as God's sub-governors does not permit the irresponsible exploitation of nature or the uncaring abuse of its resources. God's assignment to us to take dominion over the earth requires us to function as responsible stewards. Stewardship means that God has appointed us as "lords" over all things except ourselves. The responsibility for the care of the earth rests with us as an assignment from God. Although the earth belongs to the Lord (Ps. 24:1), he has given us responsibility for the land, the air, the waters, and all creatures. Our custodianship also includes responsibility for our abilities and possessions.

Most important, God has made us trustees of the gospel—the Lord calls us to treasure, to guard, and to proclaim the good news of God's saving love in Jesus Christ (I Cor. 4:1-2; Eph. 3:2; Col. 1:25; Tit. 1:7). Paul points out: "God . . . reconciled us to himself through Christ, and has given us the ministry of reconciliation; that is, in Christ God was reconciling the world to himself . . . and entrusting the message of reconciliation to us. So we are ambassadors for Christ" (II Cor. 5:17-20). As stewards of God's reconciling love, we stand accountable to God for our trusteeship of the gospel of grace (Matt. 20:8; Luke 12:42; 16:1-8).

Jesus reiterated a fundamental principle for those in positions of stewardship responsibility when he reminded us that the greatest are those who serve (Mark 10:43-44; Luke 22:26). True stewards show concern for the well-being of everything under their care; unfaithful stewards exploit their authority (see Ezek. 34:1-10). In 1972, four years after the uniting conference of 1968, the General Conference of The United Methodist Church adopted a new statement of *Social Principles,* which was revised in 1976. It contains the following affirmation: "All creation is the Lord's and we are responsible for the ways in which we use and abuse it. Water, air, soil, minerals, energy resources, plants, animal life, and space are to be valued and conserved because they are God's creation and not solely because they are useful to human beings" (BOR, 1988, 16). The high calling to take dominion over the earth requires us to obey the principles and commands of God and to seek God's will for the earth and for society.

## 3. THE PURPOSE OF CREATION

We cannot discover God's plan for the creation through rational explanations alone. As far as reason goes, it serves us well. But we can gain a *theological* understanding of the creation only from the Bible. The

Christian doctrine of creation is based on divine revelation, not on philosophical theories, scientific conjecture, or sociological surveys. Emil Brunner (*The Christian Doctrine of Creation and Redemption* [Philadelphia: Westminster Press, 1952], 39-40) suggested a fitting analogy that contrasts the scientific and theological explanations of the creation:

> How can we combine the chemical analysis of a painted canvas with the aesthetic judgment of this canvas as a work of art? Obviously the two are mutually exclusive, because the two subjects are on different planes. Where the chemist only sees the various elements of a chemical mixture, the artist sees a significant whole, an expression of mind and spirit.

Without the benefit of the biblical revelation, we can only speculate about the purpose of the world God has created. The book of Hebrews declares, "By faith we understand that the worlds were prepared by the word of God, so that what is seen was made from things that are not visible" (Heb. 11:3). In view of the numerous conflicting and speculative cosmologies, United Methodists affirm that Scripture stands as "the primary source and criterion for Christian doctrine" (*Discipline*, 81).

Scripture does not tell us *how* or *when* the earth was created, but it does affirm that God is the creator and that he created with a purpose. Ancient Israel was not so much interested in the *method* of creation as in God's *intent* for the world. If the Bible had presented the story of creation in twentieth-century scientific categories, Scripture would have been meaningless to people for many centuries. The biblical account of creation does not give a precise scientific explanation of the origin of the universe; Scripture opens to us a theological view of the creation in language that can be understood in every generation of history. A study of the whole of Scripture reveals a number of purposes for the creation.

*(a) God created the world as an expression of his love.* The following statement in United Methodism's *Book of Discipline* affirms God's purpose in creation: "The created order is designed for the well-being of all creatures and as the place of human dwelling in covenant with God" (*Discipline*, 42). God, who is absolutely wise, powerful, and good, created a world that reflects his love, a world he designed to function for his glory as a demonstration of his caring for humankind.

It is the character of love to share what one is and what one has. God purposed in and through the creation to bring into being those upon whom he could lavish benefits and blessings. Accordingly, God originated a stunningly wonderful cosmos, and the man and the woman were the highest objects of God's affection and creative genius. God wills to glorify himself as the gracious God who created an arena in which he could lavish upon us his holy love.

*(b) The creation displays the evidence of God's existence and glory.* God has not left himself without a witness to his existence. All the creation declares God's majesty (Pss. 8:1-9; 148:1-10). David wrote:

> The heavens are telling the glory of God;
>   and the firmament proclaims his handiwork.
> Day to day pours forth speech,
>   and night to night declares knowledge.
> There is no speech, nor are there words;
>   their voice is not heard;
> yet their voice goes out through all the earth,
>   and their words to the end of the world. (Ps. 19:1-2)

Paul contended that humankind has no excuse for denying God, because the natural order bears witness to his reality. "Ever since the creation of the world [God's] eternal power and divine nature, invisible though they are, have been understood and seen through the things he has made" (Rom. 1:20; also see Ps. 97:6). The creation speaks an eloquent universal language that testifies to God's existence, power, and love.

To be sure, we cannot know the nature and character of God without his revelation of himself in the incarnation of Jesus Christ. But the created order does point to the reality of a creator. Sensitive souls, with or without the benefit of revelation, perceive that the universe proclaims that God exists. The following hymn captures this thought in verse:

> Sing praise to God who reigns above,
> The God of all creation,
> The God of power, the God of love,
> The God of our salvation.
> With healing balm my soul is filled
> And every faithless murmur stilled:
> To God all praise and glory.
> (Johann J. Schütz; see *UMH*, 126)

God intended that the wonder and beauty of the creation turn our thoughts and hearts to him, the author and sustainer of all that exists. English poet Henry Francis Lyte wrote, "Earth is His altar: Nature there her daily tribute pays; / The elements upon Him wait; the seasons roll His praise" ("The Unknown God").

*(c) God created the world for our physical sustenance and pleasure.* God invested the earth with a great variety of physical benefits given for our survival and our happiness. Psalm 136 expresses a magnificent tribute of praise to God for his works in creation and in history. In that psalm the writer thanks God for the nourishment he so generously supplies for all (Ps. 136:25). God provides

us with food, minerals, seasons, and astonishing varieties of natural resources. In the biblical creation account, we read that God spoke to the first man and woman, saying, "I have given you every plant yielding seed that is upon the face of all the earth, and every tree with seed in its fruit; you shall have them for food" (Gen. 1:29). Paul told his hearers, "[God] has not left himself without a witness in doing good—giving you rains from heaven and fruitful seasons, and filling you with food and your hearts with joy" (Acts 14:17).

God intends for us to receive the provisions of nature with gratitude. As a recognition of God's gift of daily food, Christians traditionally offer thanks before partaking of the meal God has supplied. And the Church in formal worship instinctively acknowledges God as the source of our physical nourishment.

> I sing the goodness of the Lord,
> Who filled the earth with food,
> Who formed the creatures thru the Word,
> And then pronounced them good.
> Lord, how thy wonders are displayed,
> Where'er I turn my eye,
> If I survey the ground I tread,
> Or gaze upon the sky.
> (Isaac Watts; see *UMH*, 152)

Jesus told us that God, in loving provision for humankind, makes the sun rise on the evil and on the good and sends rain on the righteous and on the unrighteous (Matt. 5:45).

*(d) God's final goal for creation lies beyond this present world.* With respect to humankind, the kingdom of God begins in time, but it continues on into the future beyond this immediate life. Although the present world is splendidly awesome, the biblical revelation tells us that

the creation will reach its ultimate consummation only in eternity. *The United Methodist Hymnal* contains a section titled "A New Heaven and a New Earth," dealing with such themes as the Lord's return and the completion of creation (*UMH*, 700-734).

According to Scripture, Jesus Christ is both Alpha and Omega, the beginning and the end of history as we know it now (Rev. 1:8; 21:6; 22:13). Christ's kingdom transcends the present world; God has established a kingdom that will have no end (Isa. 9:7; Dan. 2:44; Luke 1:33; II Pet. 1:11; Rev. 11:15). God purposes, in "the fullness of time, to gather up all things in [Jesus Christ], things in heaven and things on earth" (Eph. 1:10). In the meantime, the church prays as Jesus instructed:

> Your kingdom come.
> Your will be done,
>     on earth as it is in heaven.
> (Matt. 6:10)

The incarnation of Jesus Christ fulfilled the *beginning* of the promised kingdom, so long prophesied in the Old Testament (Matt 3:2; 4:17; Mark 1:15). God sent his Son into the world for the primary mission of redeeming the human family, which is captive to sin and which can be restored to fellowship with God only through grace. This kingdom is not an earthly kingdom; it is eternal. The book of Revelation tells of the time when:

> The kingdom of the world has
>     become the kingdom of our Lord
> and of his Messiah,
> and he will reign forever and ever.
> (Rev. 11:15)

Our world now, obviously, suffers from numerous disorders that have resulted from the Fall. The earth, in its present state, reflects only dimly the world God created in the beginning and the new age that will come in the future (TJW, 166-67). The gospel of grace witnesses to the good news that, in spite of human rebellion, one day God's purposes will be fully realized, and God will establish an eternal kingdom in completeness and perfection.

# Chapter II

# SIN

*By nature ye are wholly corrupted;*
*by grace ye shall be wholly renewed.*
—John Wesley

*I*n the Bible the narrative of creation immediately
leads into an account of sin's intrusion into human
affairs. Historically, the church has referred to the
disobedience of the original man and woman and its
consequent disruption of God's plan as "the Fall." As is
the case with the Christian doctrine of creation, we
understand sin not through philosophical speculation,
but in the light of biblical revelation. Scripture gives us
a true picture of human nature, and no realistic
consideration of humankind is possible without taking
into account what Christian theology calls "original
sin."

Original sin refers to the universal disposition of us all
to seek our own will instead of God's will and to replace
the worship of God with humanly devised substitutes.
For many centuries, theologians have spoken of this
sinful condition as "total depravity." Total depravity
does not signify that we are as entirely sinful as we can
become, nor does it imply that in our natural state we are
unable to perform kind or generous acts. Total depravity
means that sin's harmful consequences reach into every
aspect of our nature and taint human intellect, emotion,

and will. The *Encyclopedia of World Methodism* (I, 576) states, "There is a gravitational pull away from God. This mysterious pulling away calls for a distinctive kind of inner transformation." Original sin does not refer so much to specific acts of sin as to our sinful *condition* (ENNT, Rom. 6:6). Sin's source lies not so much outside us as within us (see JWMT, 27-35).

The Articles of Religion of The United Methodist Church contain clear statements confessing the reality of moral depravity: "Original sin . . . is the corruption of the nature of every man, that naturally is engendered of the offspring of Adam, whereby man is very far gone from original righteousness, and of his own nature inclined to evil, and that continually" (*Discipline*, 62). A parallel expression of the sinful human condition appears in the confession of faith that United Methodism adopted from the Evangelical United Brethren Church: "We believe man is fallen from righteousness and, apart from the grace of our Lord Jesus Christ, is destitute of holiness and inclined to evil. Except a man be born again, he cannot see the Kingdom of God. In his own strength, without divine grace, man cannot do good works pleasing and acceptable to God" (*Discipline*, 71). These articles of belief accord with the Bible, which unremittingly accents the seriousness of sin.

The Christian gospel makes sense only in the context of the spiritual deprivation that infects us all. The reality of sin and the desperate spiritual condition of each one of us constitute the reason for Christ's incarnation and sacrificial death. The following adage was common in the apostolic church: "The saying is sure and worthy of full acceptance, that Christ Jesus came into the world to save sinners" (I Tim. 1:15). Reflecting on the gospel of grace, Martin Luther rightly said, "The recognition of sin is the beginning of salvation."

# 1. THE BIBLICAL ACCOUNT OF THE FALL

*(a) God's original plan for humankind.* The writer of Genesis tells that God placed the first man and woman in the garden of Eden, a paradise of perfection (Gen. 2:15). Adam and Eve were themselves in a state of flawless purity—they lived in harmony with God. No barriers existed between the first humans and their creator; they lived in constant awareness of him. Truth and honesty characterized their relationship with God. They knew no guilt, and they had nothing to hide. The writer of Genesis symbolized their perfect fellowship with the Lord by stating that regularly the man and the woman communed with God in the "cool of the day" (Gen. 3:8).

In addition to knowing God, the man and the woman enjoyed an unblemished relationship with each other. Their fellowship was not marred by the obstacles of selfishness or deceit. The harmony between male and female beautifully expressed the complementary nature of the two genders God created. The writer of Genesis symbolized this openness between the man and the woman by stating, "And the man and his wife were both naked, and were not ashamed" (Gen. 2:25).

Humankind also enjoyed absolute harmony with the natural environment. God positioned the man and the woman above all other creatures, a fact illustrated by Adam's naming of the animals (Gen. 1:28; 2:19-20). The earth was free from thorns, terror, sin, pollution, and death. Adam and Eve ruled over the natural order, and it served their needs in every way. God gave the first humans meaningful assignments: They were to till the ground and to populate the earth with their progeny. As custodians of the natural order, the man and the woman acted as responsible trustees in their ecological care-taking. So long as Adam and Eve trusted God they were free for him, for each other, and for the world.

*(b) The misuse of freedom.* God asked only one condition for the perpetual continuation of this blissful state: obedience. God permitted the man and the woman access to everything except one tree. God made clear his will: "You may freely eat of every tree of the garden; but of the tree of the knowledge of good and evil you shall not eat, for in the day that you eat of it you shall die" (Gen. 2:16-17). God wanted Adam and Eve to obey him, not because they had to do so, but because they chose to do so.

Scripture emphasizes the fact that no relationship can be authentic and genuine without the free commitment of both parties of the relationship. When Jesus said, "You shall love the Lord your God with all your heart, and with all your soul, and with all your strength, and with all your mind" (Luke 10:27), it is obvious that we can choose *not* to do so. The liturgy of The United Methodist Church contains the following question for those desiring to become members: "Do you promise, according to the grace given you, to keep God's holy will and commandments and walk in the same all the days of your life as *faithful members* of Christ's holy church?" (*UMH*, 47). We are not free in our devotion *to* God unless we are also free to turn *from* God.

God invested humankind with moral accountability. Not to the beasts, but only to the man and the woman did God give directions, warnings, and promises (Gen. 2:15-17). In the last day, God will not judge inanimate objects, the plants, or the animals. But God will judge persons, and with perfect judgment (Rom. 2:16; see also Matt. 25:31-32; Acts 17:31; Rom. 14:12; II Cor. 5:10; Heb. 9:27; II Pet. 2:9; 3:7; I John 4:17; Jude 14, 15; Rev. 20:12).

In the creation story, God told the man and the woman what they *should* do and what they should *not* do (Gen. 2:15-17; see also Gal. 5:19-26). Positively, the Lord has given us instructions regarding the actions that honor and please him. These laws work for human good and for God's honor. Negatively, God forbids certain actions, attitudes, and choices. God's commandments are not arbitrary. With perfect wisdom God defined good and bad conduct. Obedience to his instruction always leads to our happiness and to social harmony. Disobedience to God's laws dishonors God and brings tragedy to us and to our neighbors. Neither the passing of time nor changing cultural environments alter the eternal validity of God's commandments. Those who distrust God find his laws restrictive; those who trust God discover that his commands are not burdensome (I John 5:3).

Through the presence of the tree of the knowledge of good and evil God sought to prove the love and trust of the man and the woman for their Creator. Maturity comes only through testing. The presence of temptation can function as an occasion to stumble or as an opportunity to grow (I Cor. 10:13; Heb. 2:18; James 1:2-3, 12; II Pet. 2:9; Rev. 3:10). The decision of Adam and Eve to disobey God was more than a decision to break a commandment. Their disobedience constituted a choice regarding their personal relationship with God (Gen. 3:6). The essence of sin lies in our denying or refusing the absolute dominion of God. In disobeying God, the man and the woman placed their wishes above the stated wishes of their Maker. They elevated themselves above God, and such is the nature of sin. Putting our wishes ahead of God constitutes the most serious and frequent expression of sin. John Wesley's sermon "Original Sin" speaks to this point:

> We have set up our idols in our hearts; and to these we bow down and worship them: We worship ourselves, when we pay that honour to ourselves which is due to God only. Therefore all pride is idolatry; it is ascribing to ourselves

THE GOSPEL OF GRACE

what is due to God alone. And although pride was not made for man, yet where is the man that is born without it? But hereby we rob God of his unalienable right, and idolatrously usurp his glory. (WJWJ, VI, 60)

The man and the woman wanted their way more than God's way. Disobedience to God disrupted the perfect relationships that Adam and Eve enjoyed with God, each other, and the natural order (Gen. 3:1-24).

*(c) The universal spread of sin.* Sin tends to generate still more sin. Scripture tells us that sin immediately pushed out in widening circles, infecting every future generation of the human family (Rom. 5:12-21). David declared an undeniable truth regarding the pervasive and comprehensive reach of evil:

> They have all gone astray, they
> are all alike perverse;
> there is no one who does good,
> no, not one.
> (Ps. 14:3)

This fact brings us back to the doctrine of original sin: We are all born with a bent toward self-will and wrong moral choices (Gen. 6:5; Ps. 53:3; Prov. 20:9; Isa. 53:6; 64:6; Rom. 3:23; I John 1:8).

Paul underscored a profound truth when he wrote, "All have sinned and fall short of the glory of God" (Rom. 3:23). By that statement the apostle doubtless had in mind the tragic fact that sin betrays God's glory, which was included in the image God imparted to the first man and woman. Due to sin the glory of God departed from Adam and Eve. In his treatise *Original Sin*, John Wesley stated, "Man was created looking directly to God, as his last end; but, falling into sin, he fell off from God, and turned to himself. . . . And this is the case of all men in their natural state: They seek not God, but themselves" (WJWJ, IX, 456).

Sin hinders us from the life God intends for us to live. The magnitude of sin is so monstrous because in turning from God we betray and pervert the glory God gave us in creation, and we profane the attributes through which God purposed for us to honor his name. Sin has produced a trail of pain, suffering, and death to which all humankind is now subject. "Sin came into the world through one man, and death came through sin, and so death spread to all because all have sinned" (Rom. 5:12). Sin is pervasive, and sin is universal. We all need redemption. There are no exceptions (Rom. 3:9; 5:12; 7:14; Gal. 3:22).

## 2. THE ANATOMY OF SIN

*(a) The deceptive nature of sin.* One of sin's characteristics is its deception. It entices us with the promise of satisfaction, and it blinds us to its destructive consequences. While righteousness is founded on truth, sin arises out of falsehood. Scripture refers to Satan as a liar and a deceiver. Yet Satan sometimes boasts that he is a revealer of new truth (Gen. 3:5; Matt. 4:6; II Cor. 2:11; 11:14). In the Genesis account of the Fall, the tempter lied, "You will not die; for God knows that when you eat of [the forbidden tree] your eyes will be opened, and you will be like God, knowing good and evil" (Gen. 3:4-5). Temptation arises out of the false theory that the more control God has in our lives, the less free and happy we shall become. The serpent falsely asserted that God's withholding the forbidden fruit promoted God's plan to deprive humankind of privilege, knowledge, and pleasure. The tempter suggested rivalry between humankind and God.

Satan utilizes deceit because sin, when viewed

objectively, becomes shortsighted and absurdly illogical. Sin was, and is, irrational, stupid, inexplicable, and foolhardy. Paul quite appropriately speaks of the *mystery* of evil (II Thess. 2:7). We cannot give any reasonable explanation for why Adam and Eve fell into sin any more than we can explain our own sinning. Why would Adam and Eve believe the tempter rather than God? Why would they exchange the astounding blessings of their Maker for the hollow lies of the tempter? Adam and Eve had no cause to doubt God; they had every reason to trust him.

Sin's pernicious promises and gilded guarantees inevitably produce disappointment and unhappiness. Sin appears harmless, even attractive; but it always brings destruction. Mary Howitt communicated both the deception and the danger of sin in her famous nursery rhyme *The Spider and the Fly*:

> "Will you walk into my parlor?" said the spider to the fly;
> " 'Tis the prettiest little parlor that ever you did spy."

Sin blinds us to spiritual truth and offers some temporary pleasure or reward. But it draws us into its web and leads to our hurt (Deut. 28:29; Ps. 35:6; 82:5; Prov. 4:19; Isa. 59:9; Jer. 23:12; Matt. 15:14; II Pet. 2:15; I John 1:6). Thomas De Witt Talmage once remarked, "Sin may open bright as the morning, but it will end dark as night."

Sin often works its way even into religion. Swedish theologian Gustaf Aulen offers the following perceptive analysis of religion in the service of sin.

> It might be assumed that seeking after the divine, after God, would be the very opposite of sinful egocentricity. If, however, this seeking after God is in the interest of making God serve one's own ego and to secure something for one's own personal benefit by divine help, this does not imply a

turning away from sin, but rather that sin here is present in its most sublimated and deceptive form. (*The Faith of the Christian Church* [Philadelphia: The Muhlenberg Press, 1962], 235)

It was "religion" that crucified Jesus, and Christ's most damaging detractors often work in and through ecclesiastical activities. It was certainly true in biblical times, and it remains true in our own day.

Jesus leveled the charge of gross spiritual blindness against certain of his contemporaries who were religious leaders:

Why do you not understand what I say? It is because you cannot accept my word. You are from your father the devil, and you choose to do your father's desires. He was a murderer from the beginning and does not stand in the truth, because there is no truth in him. When he lies, he speaks according to his own nature, for he is a liar and the father of lies. But because I tell the truth, you do not believe me. (John 8:43-45)

The truth of the gospel stands antithetical to the mystery of evil. Light and darkness, and holiness and sin, shall forever remain opposed, and they cannot be reconciled. When the blind lead the blind, they both fall into a pit (Matt. 15:14). Some prefer darkness to light because they want their own way rather than God's way (Matt. 6:23; John 1:5; 3:19).

Scripture teaches us that sin's activity leads to exchanging the truth of God for a lie (Rom. 1:18, 25). Sin causes light to become darkness; always a refusal to love and obey the truth leads to embracing a lie and falling into spiritual blindness (II Thess. 2:10-12). When the New Testament speaks of putting off the old nature, it does so in the context of putting away falsehood and accepting truth (Rom. 13:12; Eph. 4:25; I Thess. 5:1-11). Jesus declared, "I am the way, and the truth, and the life. No one comes to the Father except through me" (John 14:6). We find ultimate truth in Jesus Christ (John 1:14; 18:37).

One of the notable characteristics of sin's deception is that it leads to self-deception; we find it difficult to admit that we are sinners or that we have sinned. Contemporary society goes to great lengths to avoid admitting its wrong. Sin is subtle, and we have devised clever ways to justify our transgressions. Someone has satirized, "People are no longer sinful, they are only immature or underprivileged or frightened, or more particularly, sick." From ancient times to the present, people tend to justify their wrongdoing and resent others who remind them of God's standard of truth and conduct. A seventeenth-century clergyman astutely observed, "Between these two, the denying of sins, which we have done, and the bragging of sins, which we have not done, what a space, what a compass is there, for millions of millions of sins!"

Commenting on the human tendency toward self-justification, the apostle Peter pointed out, "God opposes the proud, but gives grace to the humble" (I Pet. 5:5). In a similar vein, the apostle John declared, "If we confess our sins, he who is faithful and just will forgive us our sins and cleanse us from all unrighteousness. If we say that we have not sinned, we make him a liar, and his word is not in us" (I John 1:9-10).

Before his departure, Jesus plainly told us that one of the ministries of the Holy Spirit is to convince the world about its sin (John 16:8). Sin is indeed subtle, and our capacity for self-justification is enormous. But unless we confess our sins and rely wholly upon grace for our salvation, we remain separated from God. The Scottish essayist Thomas Carlyle noted that the deadliest sin is the consciousness of no sin.

*(b) The relational aspect of sin.* We cannot properly understand sin except in reference to God. Secular governments speak of crime; psychologists speak of personality disorders; philosophers speak of unethical decisions; artists speak of bad taste; sociologists speak of abnormal behavior. But Scripture speaks of sin in terms of our relationship with *God.* David the psalmist highlighted an important truth when he confessed to the Lord: "Against you, you alone, have I sinned, / and done what is evil in your sight" (Ps. 51:4).

Sometimes people incorrectly attribute sin to our finite existence as human beings. Following the worldview of such philosophers as Plato and Plotinus, this way of thinking incorrectly equates sin with human finitude or bodily appetites. This outlook contends that the experience of physical birth brings one into contact with sin. Such thinking stems from ancient Gnosticism, a philosophy that locates sin in material things, especially the flesh. This viewpoint overlooks the biblical teaching that God pronounced his creation of the world and humankind "very good." Sin stems not from our humanity or our flesh, but from the insubordinate use of our God-given freedom and capacities.

We must also say that sin is not primarily breaking a law, transgressing a commandment, or holding wrong theological opinions. Although sin may well express itself in these ways, the essence of sin involves a personal choice to put self ahead of God. When the man and the woman attempted to "be like God" (Gen. 3:5) they tried to leap to the level of their Creator. Theologically, there is no difference between the worship of self and the worship of a stone idol.

*(c) The crippling consequences of sin.* Sin renders us incapable of reaching God through our own moral

achievements. We must rely entirely on God's grace for our redemption from sin. John and Charles Wesley reaffirmed the conviction of the Protestant Reformers that we are helpless to earn salvation through human striving. Article IX of United Methodism's Confession of Faith states: "We believe we are never accounted righteous before God through our works or merit, but that penitent sinners are justified or accounted righteous before God only by faith in our Lord Jesus Christ" (*Discipline*, 71).

United Methodism's Articles of Religion state this conviction in much the same language: "We are accounted righteous before God only for the merit of our Lord and Saviour Jesus Christ, by faith, and not for our own works or deservings" (*Discipline*, 63). The belief in salvation by grace alone, apart from human merit, stands out as one of the most fundamental teachings of the Bible (Rom. 3:20; Gal. 2:16; Eph. 2:8-9; II Tim. 1:9; Tit. 3:5).

John Wesley's longest theological treatise (275 pages) discusses the doctrine of sin. The substance of that work—*The Doctrine of Original Sin, According to Scripture, Reason, and Experience*—concludes: "Man, in all his natural state, is altogether corrupt . . . in his understanding, his will, his affections, his conscience, and his memory" (WJWJ, IX, 443). In a widely circulated sermon titled *Original Sin*, John Wesley offered this advice:

> Know your disease! Know your cure! Ye were born in sin: therefore, 'ye must be born again,' born of God. By nature ye are wholly corrupted: by grace ye shall be wholly renewed. In Adam ye all died: in the second Adam, in Christ, ye all are made alive. (SSS, II, 225)

All people, even the most respectable ones, need to pray, "Take away our bent to sinning" (Charles Wesley, "Love Divine, All Loves Excelling"; see *UMH*, 384). We are not sinners because we commit acts of sin. We commit acts of sin because we are sinners.

In 1760, Philip William Otterbein, drawing upon his German Reformed background, preached a sermon stating that everyone languishes in the grip of original sin and that each person needs a redeemer. Said Otterbein: "All of us lie under this death since the fall. Our first parents fell away from God and thus necessarily into this death. We come from Adam, hence we lie with him in the same corruption and under the same judgment" (PWO, 79).

The Methodist Protestant Church also held views about original sin that were identical to those expressed in the present official documents of The United Methodist Church (*Constitution and Discipline of the Methodist Protestant Church* [Baltimore: Board of Publications of the Methodist Protestant Church, 1936], 36-37).

We sin because we will to do so, and we sin because we must do so—our fallen natures have brought us into bondage. We cannot forgive ourselves, restore ourselves, or sanctify ourselves. Classical theology has assumed that, without divine assistance, humankind is incapable of both truth and of good. Methodist theology succinctly articulates this basic biblical theme: We are saved by grace alone, through faith, apart from the works of the law, unto holiness and good works (see *Discipline*, 63, 71, 72). United Methodism's Articles of Religion echo the gratitude that every justified sinner feels: "Wherefore, that we are justified by faith, only, is a most wholesome doctrine, and very full of comfort" (*Discipline*, 63).

## 3. THE EFFECTS OF SIN

(a) *Sin and separation from God*. After their sinful disobedience, Adam and Eve immediately experienced a broken relationship with God. At the time of their daily rendezvous with God, they sought to hide from his presence (Gen. 3:8). Their former delight in communing with God gave way to dread and anxiety. They knew shame, guilt, anger, estrangement, and fear. Eventually sin leads to spiritual blindness and moral confusion, and separation from God's blessing.

A classic illustration of spiritual blindness surfaced among the first-century Pharisees who listened to what Jesus said, but could not comprehend the ideas he taught. They had become deaf and blind to the truth. We can understand the spiritual truth in the Bible only as the Holy Spirit gives assistance and opens our eyes. Without the enlightenment of the Holy Spirit, the unregenerate mind cannot grasp the gospel of grace. "Those who are unspiritual do not receive the gifts of God's Spirit, for they are foolishness to them, and they are unable to understand them because they are spiritually discerned" (I Cor. 2:14). Paul declared, "The god of this world has blinded the minds of the unbelievers, to keep them from seeing the light of the gospel of the glory of Christ" (II Cor. 4:4).

Theologian Bernard Ramm writes about the spiritual blindness caused by sin:

> When our minds are blinded by the god of this world, everything we read in the New Testament may be equivocated, e.g., "we are not sure of the Greek," "there is a parallel in the mystery cults to this," "this is a piece of Judean tradition," "this is but Paul's imagination," or, "this is a later churchly interpolation." Then, in the midst of our equivocations, God speaks: Let there be light! Immediately this creaturely equivocation ceases; unbelief burns itself out in a moment; and there before the eyes of our hearts stands Jesus Christ giving the light of the knowledge of the glory of

God. (*The Witness of the Spirit: An Essay on the Contemporary Relevance of the Internal Witness of the Holy Spirit* [Grand Rapids: Eerdmans, 1959], 43-44)

Those who surrender themselves to God and follow faithfully the teachings of Scripture receive the help of the Holy Spirit, who enables them to discern truth and error and leads them to a knowledge of God.

In spite of their hiding, their confusion, and their estrangement from God, the Lord came to Adam and Eve, seeking communication with them. It is important to remember that God took the initiative to approach the man and the woman. And God came not in wrath; God sought them in redeeming love. Again and again in Scripture we see illustrations of humankind's fleeing from God and God's faithful calling to us in our separation. The loving God ever seeks us, even in our sin (Matt. 18:12; Luke 15:4; 19:10). Such is the gospel of grace.

Sin does have consequences, of course, even when forgiven. Someone has said that we are free to make choices, but we are not free from the consequences of our choices. Because of sin, Adam and Eve forfeited their place in the Garden of Eden. The Lord placed "the cherubim, and a sword flaming and turning to guard the way to the tree of life" (Gen. 3:24). This symbolism suggests that God protects the tree of life from human initiative. We are reconciled to God, not through our means or efforts, but through God's grace.

*(b) Sin and the disorder of society.* The Fall also damaged human relationships. The man and the woman covered themselves with fig leaves, a symbol that they were no longer open to each other as they once were (Gen 3:7). Adam blamed Eve for his own disobedience (Gen. 3:12). Later, Cain killed Abel, denying that he had any responsibility for his brother (Gen. 4:1-9). Sin has caused us to look upon our neighbors not as "thous," but as

"its"—objects to be used and exploited for our own advantage.

The story of the tower of Babel (Gen. 11:1-9) symbolizes our trust in human effort to lift us to our highest potential. The confusion of languages illustrates the inability of people to live together in harmony when they set aside their dependence on God and seek to construct their own humanly designed social order. In our desire to become equal to God and "to make a name for ourselves" we hurt other people, and we misuse God's gifts. A relatively short time after the Fall, "The LORD saw that the wickedness of humankind was great in the earth, and that every inclination of the thoughts of their hearts was only evil continually" (Gen. 6:5). It has been astutely observed that the doctrine of original sin is the easiest Christian doctrine to verify with empirical evidence!

In addition to affecting relationships with God and with fellow human beings, the Fall also had a bearing on the natural environment. This consequence is summarized in the following passage, in which God said:

> Cursed is the ground because of you;
> in toil you shall eat of it all the
> days of your life;
> thorns and thistles it shall bring
> forth for you;
> and you shall eat the plants of
> the field.
> By the sweat of your face
> you shall eat bread
> until you return to the ground.
> (Gen. 3:17-19)

The Fall resulted in the resistance of the earth to our efforts to master it. As a consequence of the Fall, we no longer have freedom from floods, earthquakes, droughts, and hurricanes.

In turn, sin now takes an enormous toll with respect to how we treat the earth. The atrocities we perpetrate against our natural environment stem from our selfish quest for self-advantage. We ruthlessly exploit and pollute our world, with little thought for future generations. R. H. Dana lamented, "O sin, what hast thou done to this fair earth!" Happily, though, Paul tells us that one day "the creation itself will be set free from its bondage to decay and will obtain the freedom of the glory of the children of God" (Rom. 8:21). Christians look forward to the future when God will establish "a new heaven and a new earth" (Isa. 65:17; II Pet. 3:13; Rev. 21:1).

*(c) The continuing tragedy of sin.* United Methodism's *Book of Discipline* summarizes the biblical doctrine of original sin: "As sinful creatures . . . we have broken [God's] covenant, become estranged from God, wounded ourselves and one another, and wreaked havoc throughout the natural order. We stand in need of redemption" (*Discipline,* 42). The effects of sin touch us at every point of our human experience—spiritually, interpersonally, and environmentally.

Today some argue that the church should never say anything uncomplimentary concerning human nature or about people's unrighteous life-styles. Citing the need for tolerance, they contend that we should preach only that God is love and that we should not speak of sin or judgment. To be sure, God is loving—the Bible stresses that fact in many places. But to speak of God's love to the neglect of the reality of sin and judgment leads to a one-sided gospel.

In a letter written in 1750, John Wesley noted:

> I see a danger you are in, which perhaps you do not see yourself. Is it not most pleasing to me as well as you to be

always preaching the love of God? And is there not a time when we are peculiarly led thereto, and find a peculiar blessing therein? Without doubt so it is. But yet it would be utterly wrong and unscriptural to preach of nothing else. . . . I scarce ever spoke more earnestly here of the love of God in Christ than last night; but it was after I had been tearing the unawakened in pieces. Go thou and do likewise. (LJW, III, 34)

If we speak of Christ as savior, we must understand that humankind needs saving. We need no savior if we have no sin. John Wesley captured the essence of scriptural teaching when he declared, "We know no gospel without salvation from sin" (LJW, VI, 327). Unless we are saved from our sins, we will die in our sins. And in dying outside God's grace we are permanently separated from him (*Discipline*, 67; EWM, I, 701; *UMH*, 413; Matt. 25:32).

We err if we fail to preach about sin and judgment. We also err if we focus on sin to the extent that we obscure the good news that Jesus Christ came into the world to save sinners (I Tim. 1:15). Wesleyan theology points up the biblical truth that God's grace goes deeper than the stain of sin. Christ "gave himself for our sins to set us free from the present evil age" (Gal. 1:4). Peter wrote, "[Christ] himself bore our sins in his body on the cross, so that, free from sins, we might live for righteousness; by his wounds you have been healed" (I Pet. 2:24; see also Rev. 1:5-6). Jesus Christ breaks the power of canceled sin, sets free the prisoners to sin, and liberates us to live godly lives in the present age (Tit. 2:11-14).

United Methodist hymnody contains numerous confessions of sin and prayers for God's forgiveness and cleansing. The following hymn by Charles Wesley expresses an awareness of sin and the promise of God to pardon those who turn to him for grace and power.

Other refuge have I none,
Hangs my helpless soul on thee;
Leave, ah! leave me not alone,
Still support and comfort me.
All my trust on thee is stayed,
All my help from thee I bring;
Cover my defenseless head
With the shadow of thy wing.
(see *UMH*, 479)

Whatever else we say about the human condition, we must take into account our sinful condition and the fact that we need the salvation that Jesus Christ alone provides.

Sin takes many forms—some of them subtle, and some of them blatant. The British theologian J. S. Whale stated that sins consist of two types: hot-blooded sins of the flesh and cold-blooded sins of the spirit. Both expressions of sin dishonor God, and they arise out of our fallen condition. The prodigal son and the elder brother both sinned. In one case, sin exploded outwardly, and in the other case sin simmered quietly beneath the surface. Whether our sins resemble the hot-blooded sins of the prodigal son or the cold-blooded sins of the elder brother, we are sinners who need the grace of God.

Happily sin is not the final word in the Christian gospel. The grace of God is greater than our sin. John Wesley held that the three pillars of the theology of Christian experience are (1) original sin, (2) justification by faith, and (3) holiness of heart and life (LJW, IV, 146, 237). These three doctrines—sin, grace, and holiness—constitute important components in the doctrinal statements of all branches of the Christian church. The church sings:

Marvelous grace of our loving Lord,
Grace that exceeds our sin and our guilt!

> Yonder on Calvary's mount outpoured,
> There where the blood of the Lamb was spilt.
> Grace, grace, God's grace,
> Grace that will pardon and cleanse within;
> Grace, grace, God's grace,
> Grace that is greater than all our sin!
> (Julia H. Johnston; see *UMH*, 365)

Wesleyan theology offers a particularly constructive development of the biblical teaching that through the gospel of grace God offers a wonderful salvation that can lead to a genuine change for individuals and for the entire globe.

# Chapter III

# GRACE

*Salvation's free, we tell! we tell!*
*Shouted the Methodist bell.*
—George W. Bungay, "The Creeds of the Bells"

A t the center of the biblical revelation stands the doctrine of grace. Grace means God's unmerited favor doing for us what we cannot do for ourselves. God's grace comes to us in many ways, and it attends us from birth to death. We depend upon grace in every aspect of our lives. Without the grace of God the cosmos itself would fly into disarray and chaos. In a couplet written "for boys and girls," John Bunyan expressed the human need for divine assistance:

Nor can a man with grace his soul inspire,
More than the candles set themselves on fire.

God's grace operates in its highest form at the point of our deepest need—deliverance from inbred sin and spiritual death (see John 1:1-17; Acts 15:11; Rom. 3:24; 5:15; 11:6; Tit. 2:11; 3:7).

Salvation is not a human achievement, but a divine work (see Rom. 3:19-26; Gal. 2:11-21; Eph. 2:8-9). Redemption does not rest upon ancestry, social class, personal effort, or the ministrations of any person or organization—it is a work of God (John 1:12-13). Through grace we find release from spiritual darkness, become reconciled to God, and participate in a new humanity (see Luke 4:18-21; II Cor. 5:17; Gal. 6:15; Eph. 2:15; 4:24; Col. 3:10). God's saving work is such a powerful force in human life that Scripture likens our experience of this grace to being raised from the dead (see Rom. 8:11; Eph. 2:1, 6; Col. 3:1). The religion of the Bible is a religion of grace, and without grace there could be no gospel and no salvation (see Acts 4:12; I Cor. 3:11).

## 1. THE PRIMACY OF GRACE IN SCRIPTURE

The doctrine of grace helps to shape our understanding of God. Scripture teaches us that in love, God graciously bestows undeserved favor upon us, doing for us what we cannot do for ourselves. Frederick W. Faber wrote of this grace:

> There's a wideness in God's mercy
> Like the wideness of the sea;
> There's a kindness in God's justice,
> Which is more than liberty.
> (see *UMH*, 121)

God's grace, if unhindered by our resistance, leads us to a personal experience of God. This saving grace continues in our lives through sanctification, which is the renewal of the image of God within us through the working of the Holy Spirit (see Rom. 6:6-17; Gal. 5:22-26; Titus 3:7-8). Grace depends on no human merit or achievement; it comes to us as an expression of God's immeasurable love for humankind.

*(a) Biblical terms for grace.* Although the Old Testament illuminates grace through a variety of illustrations, it uses two specific terms that we usually translate as "grace"—*hen* and *hesed.* These words are sometimes used to refer to relationships between people, but usually they pertain to divine-human relationships. The Hebrew word *hen* refers to the gracious action of a

superior to an inferior. The benevolent act of the more powerful on behalf of the less powerful obviously presupposes a need in the one who receives assistance. The weaker one needs help because of natural inability or unfavorable circumstances. The one who offers compassion does so voluntarily, not because the stronger one is obligated to aid the weaker, but because the stronger one acts out of compassion and love. Grace means the granting of benefit, not as a right but as a favor.

The Old Testament frequently uses the word *hen* to describe God's gracious choosing and care of Israel. For instance, we read in Jeremiah's prophecy:

> Thus says the LORD:
> The people who survived the sword
> found (grace) [*hen*] in the wilderness;
> when Israel sought for rest,
>    the LORD appeared to him
>    from far away.
> (Jer. 31:2-3)

God's demonstrations of gracious favor do not suggest a resentful or condescending attitude on the part of the benefactor. Rather, they allude to a particular action that expresses love and good will.

The other Old Testament word for grace is *hesed*, which pertains primarily to interpersonal relationships. The Hebrew word *hesed* means grace that is revealed in mercy, lovingkindness, or goodness. This word often appears in association with God's covenant with individuals and with Israel. The Old Testament contains many expressions of praise to God for God's *hesed*—his gracious steadfast love. For instance, the psalmist declares: "Because your steadfast love [*hesed*] is better than life, / my lips will praise you" (Ps. 63:3; see also

Pss. 5:7; 17:7; 26:3; 57:3; 89:1-2, 33; Lam. 3:22-23). *Hesed* emphasizes the abundance of God's provisions that he graciously bestows in unexpected ways. This grace cannot be earned. The proper response to such grace is thankful praise, holy living, and love toward neighbors. Ancient Israel exulted:

> We ponder your steadfast love [*hesed*], O God,
>     in the midst of your temple.
> Your name, O God, like your praise,
>     reaches to the ends of the earth.
> (Ps. 48:9-10)

In the New Testament, the most commonly used word for grace is *charis*. Primarily, *charis* refers to God's mercy and saving power to redeem sinful humankind. "For by grace [*charis*] you have been saved through faith, and this is not your own doing; it is the gift of God" (Eph. 2:8). The word *charis* forms the root for *charisma*, which can be translated literally "free gift of grace." For instance, Paul writes, "The wages of sin is death, but the free gift (*charisma*) of God is eternal life in Christ Jesus our Lord" (Rom. 6:23). Because the Fall rendered us spiritually powerless to redeem ourselves, we must rely completely on God's grace for our salvation (see Acts 15:11; Rom. 3:23; 5:15; 11:6; Tit. 2:11; 3:7). The parable of the prodigal son illustrates that the Father in heaven lovingly welcomes all who turn to him, and he graciously restores them.

The word *grace* also occupies a prominent place in the opening greetings and the closing benedictions of the New Testament epistles (e.g., Acts 13:43; 20:32; Rom. 1:7; 16:20; I Cor. 1:3; 16:23; II Cor. 1:2; 13:14; Gal. 1:3; 6:18; Eph. 1:2; 6:24; Phil. 1:2; 4:23; Col. 1:2; 4:18; I Thess. 1:1; 5:28; II Thess. 1:2; 3:18; I Pet. 1:2; 5:12; Rev. 22:21). Paul's letters repeatedly contrast salvation by grace with the then current, and ever-recurring, idea of justification by good works and human merit. Our reliance on the grace of God means that we surrender pride and the desire to control our own destiny. Charles Wesley captured the idea of our constant need of grace:

> Other refuge have I none,
> Hangs my helpless soul on thee;
> Leave, ah! leave me not alone,
> Still support and comfort me.
> All my trust on thee is stayed,
> All my help from thee I bring;
> Cover my defenseless head
> With the shadow of thy wing.
> (see *UMH*, 479)

Because Christians rely entirely on God's grace, one of the church's favorite blessings from New Testament times to the present is

The grace of the Lord Jesus Christ,
and the love of God,
and the communion of the Holy Spirit be with you all.
(BOS, 26)

*(b) The universal scope of grace.* We learn from Scripture that God extends grace toward *everyone*. No one stands outside the circle of God's love, and the Lord invites all people to be saved (see Luke 3:6; Acts 2:21; Rom. 5:18; 10:13; I Tim. 2:4; Tit. 2:11; II Pet. 3:9). Jesus instructed his disciples to preach the gospel of grace to Jews, Samaritans, and Gentiles (see Matt. 24:14; 28:19; Mark 13:10; Luke 24:47; Acts 1:8; Rev. 14:6). Grace alone breaks down barriers between people of different races and cultures. God continues to call those who seemingly have no interest in spiritual issues and also those who are zealously pursuing false religions. The apostle John speaks of Jesus Christ as the "true light, which

enlightens everyone" (John 1:9; see also 3:15-16; Rom. 10:12; I Tim. 2:4; II Pet. 3:9).

The Wesleyan emphasis on the call of God to all people contrasts with the view that God decrees to save some and condemn others. In Wesley's and Otterbein's days, the dominant Protestant teaching in the English-speaking world insisted that Christ's atonement was limited; allegedly Christ died only for the elect. The doctrine of predestination insisted that, before the world began, God elected some for salvation and some for damnation. A popular saying of the time was, "The saved will be saved, do what they will; the damned will be damned, do what they can." Wesleyan theology has always rejected the so-called "eternal decrees," insisting that Christ died for all.

Charles Wesley's hymns acclaim the universal offer of God's grace to everyone who will receive it.

> Thy sovereign grace to all extends,
> Immense and unconfined;
> From age to age it never ends;
> It reaches all mankind.
> Throughout the world its breadth is known,
> Wide as infinity,
> So wide it never passed by one;
> Or it had passed by me.
> (PJCW, IV, 445; see also *The Book of Hymns*, 130)

Although Christ died that all can be redeemed, not all persons will accept this grace. Christian theology distinguishes between God's universal offer of grace and *universalism*, which is the doctrine that goes beyond the biblical teaching that all *may* be saved to speculate that all *will* be saved. According to universalism, all moral creatures—angels, humans, and demons—will ultimately enjoy the benefit of salvation. Universalism holds that hell is temporary and purgative, and every person will eventually know salvation. Scripture, however, gives us a different picture from the one painted by universalism. God is indeed a God of universal grace, but some people persist in rejecting God's loving provision of salvation. God does not force us against our wills to accept his offer of salvation.

Throughout Scripture and the history of Christian doctrine runs the theme of a final judgment and permanent separation from God. Jesus said, "I came into this world for judgment" (John 9:39), and he warned that in the last day God will separate the "sheep" from the "goats" (Matt. 25:31-33). The Gospels record a good number of Jesus' references to this eternal separation (e.g., Matt. 5:22, 29; 10:28; 18:9; 23:15, 33; Mark 9:43; Luke 12:5).

United Methodism's Articles of Religion (Article X) also speak of God's final judgment (*Discipline*, 63). United Methodism's Confession of Faith states, "We believe in the resurrection of the dead; the righteous to life eternal and the wicked to endless condemnation" (Article XII, *Discipline*, 72; see EWM, I, 701).

The gospel ministry of the church appropriately stresses God's love for every person and the opportunity for all to know God through repentance and faith in Jesus Christ. Wise witnesses of God's grace will declare plainly and lovingly that whosoever will can be saved. At the same time, the faithful ministry of God's word requires us to warn of a future judgment and the possibility of permanent separation from God. We fall into hazardous speculation, however, when we pronounce *who* is saved or lost (see Matt. 7:1; Rom. 14:4, 13; I Cor. 4:5; Heb. 12:23; James 4:12). God alone is the true judge. English essayist Samuel Johnson once wisely remarked, "God himself, sir, does not propose to judge man until the end of his days."

## ۵ 2. PREVENIENT GRACE

(a) The divine initiative. Prior to our awareness of God, God prepares us to turn to him. Jesus said, "No one can come to me unless drawn by the Father who sent me" (John 6:44; see also Jer. 31:3; I John 4:10). God cultivates our hearts long before we have any inclination to turn to him. The Holy Spirit creates within us a desire for God, and this gracious activity takes place well ahead of our consciousness of his working in our lives.

Christian theology refers to this gracious activity of God as "prevenient grace." The word *prevenient* (or *preventing*) means "coming before, preceding, or antecedent." God's prevenient grace creates and prompts our spiritual desires, drawing us to faith in Jesus Christ. Through prevenient grace, God comes to us in our unregenerate state to turn our thoughts to himself and to enable us to experience him personally.

Article VIII of United Methodism's Articles of Religion speaks about the doctrine of prevenient grace:

> The condition of man after the fall of Adam is such that he cannot turn and prepare himself, by his own natural strength and works, to faith, and calling upon God; wherefore we have no power to do good works, pleasant and acceptable to God, without the grace of God by Christ preventing us, that we may have a good will, and working with us, when we have that good will. (*Discipline*, 63)

United Methodism's Confession of Faith also affirms the doctrine of prevenient grace (see *Discipline*, 68).

When United Methodists speak of prevenient grace, they underscore the biblical doctrine that we cannot save ourselves without God's intervention in our lives.

Discussing "Our Doctrinal Heritage," the United Methodist *Book of Discipline* offers the following definition of prevenient grace:

> We acknowledge God's prevenient grace, the divine love that surrounds all humanity and precedes any and all of our conscious impulses. This grace prompts our first wish to please God, our first glimmer of understanding concerning God's will, and our "first slight transient conviction" of having sinned against God.
>
> [This] grace also awakens in us an earnest longing for deliverance from sin and death and moves us toward repentance and faith. (*Discipline*, 46)

Conversion to Jesus Christ takes place only after the prior work of the Holy Spirit, who prepares us and turns our hearts toward God. We love God because God first loved us (I John 4:19).

*The United Methodist Hymnal* contains a rich section of hymns under the theme Prevenient Grace (*UMH*, 337-56). The following stanza typifies the focus of these hymns:

> I sought the Lord, and afterward I knew
> He moved my soul to seek him, seeking me.
> It was not I that found, O Savior true;
> No, I was found of thee.
> (see *UMH*, 341)

Prevenient grace manifests itself in many ways. God protects us, providentially guides us, convicts us of sin, and gives us the desire and the ability to repent and to believe (see WOS, 23).

*(b) The enlightened conscience.* One of the most obvious ways we sense the operation of prevenient grace is through the conscience (WJWJ, VII, 187). An important function of our conscience is our self-awareness with

respect to our relationship to God. Often theology refers to this self-awareness as "awakening." *Awakening* is a term used to specify the work of the Holy Spirit that arouses our awareness of our sin, our accountability before God, and our need for salvation (see WJWJ, V, 101-2).

Wesleyan theology holds the view that without God's assistance we would not be conscious of sin or of our need of grace (see LJW, VI, 239). Nor do we have any ability to turn to God on our own initiative. In one of his sermons, John Wesley gave particular attention to the work of prevenient grace in our consciences: "No man living is entirely destitute of what is vulgarly called *natural conscience*. But this is not natural; it is more properly termed *preventing grace*. Every man has a greater or less measure of this, which waiteth not for the call of man" (WJWJ, VI, 512). Wesleyan theology holds that conscience is not a natural attribute of humankind; conscience is created within us by the prior work of prevenient grace (PDL, 32-36).

Unaided human insight cannot comprehend the truth of God. Our finitude stands as a barrier between us and the knowledge of the infinite God, and our sin renders us unworthy to come into his presence. Unassisted by grace, we can only plunge into greater and greater confusion regarding spiritual reality. Only through the prior work of God can we ever come to know him (II Cor. 4:4; Eph. 4:18). According to Scripture, "Those who are unspiritual do not receive the gifts of God's Spirit, for they are foolishness to them, and they are unable to understand them because they are spiritually discerned" (I Cor. 2:14). God enables those who respond to the work of prevenient grace to grasp the truth of the gospel and the deep "mysteries of the Spirit."

John Wesley differed from his French contemporary, philosopher Jean-Jacques Rousseau, who believed that natural conscience was absolutely reliable with regard to right and wrong. Rousseau denied original sin, the need for biblical revelation, and the work of the Holy Spirit in prevenient grace. Rousseau maintained that we do not require God's assistance to reach our highest potential. Numerous people hold the same view today. But United Methodist theology recognizes both original sin and the need for grace (TRTN, 78-82). Any good within us is not a natural attribute, but a work of God.

Conscience can approve and condemn, but without the biblical revelation and the operation of God's Spirit we do not always know *what* is right or wrong. Wesleyan theology recognizes the important truth that the contents of our consciences reflect the sources that have informed them (see GFH, 431-36). Therefore, conscience can be subjective, and it is not always reliable. John Wesley declared:

> We find some who fear where no fear is; who are continually condemning themselves without cause; imagining some things to be sinful, which the Scripture nowhere condemns; and supposing other things to be their duty, which the Scripture nowhere enjoins. . . . But the extreme which is opposite to this is far more dangerous. A hardened conscience is a thousand times more dangerous than a scrupulous one. (WJWJ, VII, 191; cf. LJW, III, 157)

Unless hindered by disobedience, the work of prevenient grace through a biblically informed conscience will "shine more and more to the perfect day" (ENNT, John 1:9).

*(c) Free will and human responsibility.* Although our salvation is completely a work of grace, it involves our cooperation with God. Our appropriate response to the

work of prevenient grace includes confessing that we are guilty sinners who need God's grace to pardon us and to change our hearts. Theology in the Wesleyan tradition holds that a conviction of sin comprises an important first step toward salvation. And God gives us the ability to respond to his offer of grace. With respect to conversion, we may say, "Without God we cannot, without us God will not."

Secular thinking maintains that we should deny, ignore, or rationalize our wrongdoing. Those who do not understand the gospel of grace mistakenly advise us to shift the blame for our transgressions to circumstances, stress, society at large, inexperience, or our education (or lack of it). Some even fault Christianity for "teaching us to feel guilty." Modern secular society places great emphasis on "accepting" ourselves and others in our present state, regardless of our theological opinions or morally sinful life-styles. Such thinking contradicts the gospel, which encourages us to admit our guilt, forsake our sins, and call upon God for pardon (Luke 18:9-14).

We cannot truly be Christians unless we become willing to confess our trespasses and in penitence turn to the Lord for justifying grace (I Tim. 1:15). Prevenient grace creates new possibilities for human existence. God stirs us out of spiritual slumber and produces within us the desire and the grace to become new creations in Christ (Ezek. 11:19; II Cor. 5:17). Based on the witness of Scripture and the testimony of their own experiences, Christians sing with gratitude:

> 'Twas grace that taught my heart to fear,
> And grace my fears relieved;
> How precious did that grace appear
> The hour I first believed.
> (John Newton; see *UMH*, 378)

## 3. GROWTH IN GRACE

The word *Methodist* originated as a sarcastic term to describe John Wesley and the other members of the Holy Club for the orderly and deliberate *methods* they used in their religious quest for saving grace. From the beginning, the Methodists objected to the notion that we should wait passively, without prayer or the use of the ordinances of the church, for God to work in our lives. The early Methodists refused to accept the teaching that using religious exercises in seeking God meant that one was relying on good works instead of grace. As John Wesley contended, "God does not, will not, give that faith, unless we seek it with all diligence, in the way which he hath ordained" (WJWJ, XI, 403).

(a) *The means of grace.* In harmony with the practice of historic Christianity, Methodism encourages a disciplined Christian life. Discipline includes the diligent use of the "means of grace" (*Discipline*, 43). John Wesley categorized the means of grace under two headings—*instituted* and *prudential* (see JWTT, 130-40; WJWJ, VIII, 322-24). Listing the instituted means of grace, he included those religious exercises clearly taught in Scripture. By the prudential means of grace, Wesley meant the rules for living that reason, tradition, and experience have proved helpful for growth in holiness. To encourage the use of the means of grace, in 1743 John Wesley prepared "The General Rules of the United Societies" (see *Discipline*, 74-77). These guidelines have appeared in every Methodist *Discipline* to the present day.

John Wesley was more than a theologian and an evangelist—he was also a pastor. As a pastor, he observed the tendency of uninstructed and undisciplined converts to fall into a "wilderness state," by which he meant returning to the former ways of sin

(SSS, II, 244-63). He wrote, "I was more convinced than ever that the preaching like an apostle, without joining together those that are awakened and training them up in the ways of God, is only begetting children for [Satan]" (JJW, V, 26). Wesley tirelessly preached that God calls us to a life of disciplined Christian discipleship. As stated in United Methodism's *Book of Discipline*, "Methodists have always been strictly enjoined to maintain the unity of faith and good works through the means of grace" (*Discipline*, 48).

John Wesley explained, "By 'means of grace,' I understand outward signs, words, or actions, ordained of God, and appointed for this end, to be the ordinary channels whereby He might convey to men, preventing, justifying, or sanctifying grace" (SSS, I, 242). Wesley contended that the following "instituted means of Grace" find their source in biblical instruction: (1) prayer, (2) searching the Scriptures, (3) The Lord's Supper, (4) fasting, and (5) Christian conference (see WJWJ, VIII, 322-23). The "prudential means of grace" are not specifically set forth in Scripture, but they are "prudent" for our growth in grace. In contrast to the instituted means of grace, the prudential means of grace can vary according to changing circumstances.

The *General Rules* contain three principles:

1. *Doing no harm, avoiding evil of every kind*. A partial list of "evils," which appears in the *General Rules*, includes taking the name of God in vain, profaning the Lord's Day, the abuse of alcohol, enslaving others, dishonest business practices, tax cheating, gossiping, questionable recreational activities, needless self-indulgence, and greed.

2. *Doing as much good as possible*. Wesley describes doing good works as the "arts of holy living" (WJWJ,

VIII, 323). Under the heading of doing good, the *General Rules* speak of showing mercy to all, providing for the physical needs of the poor, witnessing in word and action to the power of the gospel, denying self for the good of others, and accepting reproach or persecution as an inevitable result of our faithfulness to Christ.

3. *By attending upon all the ordinances of God.* Specifically, the *General Rules* encourage such exercises as public worship, Bible study, holy communion, family and personal prayer, fasting, and abstinence.

Using the means of grace, of course, does not atone for any of our sins or produce merit. Christian discipline must be seen not as an end, but as *means.* When our uses of the ordinances of God lead to inward and outward holiness they profit us a great deal. But if we regard them as meritorious acts, they lead to self-deception and pride. The means of grace outlined in the *General Rules* can serve the desirable end of holiness, because serious discipleship requires disciplined living.

On examination, these *General Rules* consist largely of a string of biblical quotations, as do also the encouragements to holy living found in the hymn texts of Charles Wesley (see PDL, 25-27; TWH, 11-20). To scorn the appointed means of grace is to deny a number of God's specific commandments (SSS, I, 237-60). Although written in the eighteenth century, the *General Rules* remain astonishingly relevant today.

(b) *The freedom of grace.* Two potential errors may emerge with respect to the means of grace—undervaluing them and overvaluing them. When we undervalue discipline in the Christian life we tend to become lazy and morally lax. When we overvalue the means of grace we tend to fall into legalism and joyless religion.

It is obvious that the *General Rules* pertain to outward forms, and Christianity is an inward condition. As stated, United Methodism's *General Rules* are not inflexible. The moral law of Scripture remains unchanging, but its *application* may need adjustment according to the needs of the day. For instance, the Bible tells us to keep the Lord's Day holy, but how one applies that mandate to one's particular circumstances may vary from place to place and from time to time. In *A Plain Account of the People Called Methodists*, Wesley wrote, "We declare them all [the rules] to be merely prudential, not essential, not of divine institution. . . . We are always open to instruction; willing to be wiser every day than we were before, and to change whatever we can change for the better" (WJWJ, VIII, 254).

While the instituted means of grace come directly from Scripture, the prudential means of grace fall into a different category. So long as we do not violate the plain teaching of Scripture, we have freedom to follow the Holy Spirit as he leads us in our Christian living today. Reason and experience help us to apply what we receive from Scripture and tradition.

Without inner freedom and love, a religious exercise is by itself "a poor dead, empty thing: separate from God, it is a dry leaf, a shadow" (SSS, I, 259). John Wesley's wise counsel remains valid today:

> In using all means, seek God alone. In and through every outward thing, look singly to the *power* of His Spirit, and the *merits* of His Son. Beware you do not stick in the *work* itself; if you do, it is all lost labour. Nothing short of God can satisfy your soul. Therefore, eye Him in all, through all, and above all. (SSS, I, 259-60)

The sole purpose of Methodism's development of rules, regulations, and uses has been to aid Christians in personal growth and in ministry to the world.

The firm conviction that Christian faith and experience ought to be expressed in holy living led [Methodism's] early leaders to adopt similar patterns of ecclesiastical organization and discipline to assist Christians in spiritual growth and Christian witness. (*Discipline*, 17)

The organization and activity of the Church are not ends, but means to bring salvation to lost people, promote inward holiness, and lead to the transformation of society.

# Chapter IV

# CONVERSION

*What I feared to be parted from*
*was now a joy to surrender.*
— St. Augustine

*I*f anyone is in Christ, there is a new creation: everything old has passed away; see, everything has become new" (II Cor. 5:17). So wrote the apostle Paul, describing conversion—one of the most distinguishing doctrines of the Christian faith. The *Encyclopedia of World Methodism* (I, 576) defines conversion as "a part of God's revealed purpose to bring people, by divine grace and human response, into a conscious and life-giving relationship with God himself." Concerning this experience, John Wesley wrote, "Sin is remitted, and pardon is applied to the soul, by a divine faith wrought by the Holy Ghost, who then begins the great work of inward sanctification" (ENNT, Rom. 4:5). Conversion is the life-transforming religious experience by which we become Christians. Through conversion we participate by faith in the redemptive work of Jesus Christ, affirm his lordship, become a part of his body (the church), and begin the process of moral transformation which renews us in his image. Conversion involves the conscious decision and act of a person in which he or she turns from sin, trusts in God's grace, and begins a life of fellowship with the resurrected Lord

Jesus Christ. This change results in a new standing, a new power, and a new destiny.

Scripture teaches us that conversion is the fundamental prerequisite for entrance into the kingdom of God. Jesus said, "Truly I tell you, unless you change [Greek, "be converted"] and become like children, you will never enter the kingdom of heaven" (Matt. 18:3; see also John 3:3; Acts 3:19; 15:3; Tit. 3:5; I Pet. 1:23). Some conversions are sudden and dramatic, as was the case with Paul (Acts 9:5-6) and the Philippian jailer (Acts 16:25-32). Other conversions are unspectacular, such as we read about in Luke's accounts of the Ethiopian eunuch (Acts 8:30-38) and of Lydia (Acts 16:11-15). In Scripture, the root meaning of conversion is to turn around or to change directions. When one does turn in a new direction, the crucial matter is not how far on the road one has traveled, but the change of course that leads to a new destination.

## 1. THE NEW BIRTH

*(a) Repentance: turning from the old.* A major biblical theme pertaining to conversion is repentance. To repent means to turn from your way to God's way. The Old Testament abounds with instances of God's invitation to sinning nations to repent and change direction. The New Testament shifts the focus from national repentance to individual repentance. Both John the Baptizer and Jesus began their public ministries with the statement, "Repent, for the kingdom of heaven has come near" (Matt 3:2; 4:17).

The most common Old Testament word for repentance is *shubh,* which means "to go in the opposite direction," "to turn back," or "to change one's direction" (see I Kings 8:35; Job 36:10; Isa. 59:20; Joel 2:12-13). The principle New Testament word for repentance is *metanoia,* which means "to reverse one's course" (see Matt. 3:8; Luke 3:8; Acts 20:21; 26:20; Rom. 2:4; II Tim. 2:25). Repentance involves turning in a new direction with the whole heart.

The theme of repentance constituted a major focus of apostolic preaching. For instance, Paul declared, "While God has overlooked the times of human ignorance, now he commands all people everywhere to repent, because he has fixed a day on which he will have the world judged in righteousness" (Acts 17:30-31). And Peter echoes this fundamental message: "The Lord is . . . patient with you, not wanting any to perish, but all to come to repentance" (II Pet. 3:9). The message of the New Testament insists that one cannot participate in the kingdom of God until one is ready to forsake the old attachments to sin and self-will. The New Testament both begins and ends with a call to repent (Matt. 3:2; Rev. 3:19).

The theme of repentance has appropriately constituted an important place in the Wesleyan tradition. In his often-quoted sermon *The Scripture Way of Salvation,* John Wesley states:

> God does undoubtedly command us both to repent, and to bring forth fruits meet for repentance; which if we willingly neglect, we cannot reasonably expect to be justified at all: therefore both repentance, and fruits meet for repentance, are . . . necessary to justification. (SSS, II, 451; WJWJ, VI, 48)

Reiterating this thought, *The Book of Discipline* affirms, "Because God truly loves us in spite of our willful sin, God judges us, summons us to repentance, pardons us, receives us by that grace given to us in Jesus Christ, and gives us hope of life eternal" (*Discipline,* 42). The nineteenth-century *Cyclopaedia of Methodism* stated:

Methodists believe that in the salvation of the sinner, the Holy Spirit enlightens his understanding and causes him to see his need of a Saviour; that under this spiritual influence and power the first step is repentance, or turning from sin, the second, believing in the Lord Jesus Christ (COM, 749).

One other word about repentance needs to be emphasized: Repentance does not end at conversion. The Lord's Prayer, "forgive us our debts," indicates the need for ongoing repentance. We do not repent for sins already forgiven, of course, but we should always repent for our failure to live as obediently and faithfully as we could. Sins of commission and sins of omission need God's pardoning love. Blaise Pascal astutely observed, "There are only two kinds of men: the righteous who believe themselves sinners; the rest, sinners, who believe themselves righteous" (*Pensées*, 562).

The United Methodist service of Holy Communion contains the following call to Christians to repent:

> *Minister:* Christ our Lord invites to his table all who love him, who earnestly repent of their sin and who seek to live in peace with one another. Therefore, let us confess our sin before God and one another:
>
> *Minister and people:* Merciful God, we confess that often we have failed to be an obedient church. We have not done your will, we have rebelled against your love, we have not loved our neighbors, and we have not heard the cry of the needy. Forgive us, we pray. Free us for joyful obedience, through Jesus Christ our Lord. Amen. (BOS, 27)

Repentance involves more than regret that one is not a better person or anguish that one has to live with the consequences of one's sinful actions. Scripture speaks of a "godly grief [that] produces a repentance that leads to salvation" (II Cor. 7:10). Repentance means forsaking our sins and following Christ in full obedience. The truly repentant person acknowledges sin as an offense against God and determines to change his or her present direction. John Wesley rightly insisted, "We must repent before we can believe the gospel. We must be cut off from dependency upon ourselves before we can truly depend on Christ" (WJWJ, V, 241). We can never travel in God's ways until we turn from all paths that lead away from him.

*(b) Faith: turning to the new.* Along with repentance, faith forms an essential part of conversion. Turning *from* must be accompanied by turning *to.* The prodigal son turned away from his wayward life, and he determined to go to his father's house. Unless repentance leads to faith it remains incomplete. The noun and verb forms of the word *faith* appear about 240 times in the New Testament, and the word means "to trust" or "to place confidence in." The book of Acts sometimes refers to Christians by the term *believers*—those who have faith. In the New Testament, believing means two things: (1) the acceptance of a body of truth on the basis of apostolic testimony (for us, this means the Scriptures) and (2) a personal trust in and dependence on, Jesus Christ. Without personal faith in Jesus Christ, we cannot be saved (see John 3:15; 5:24; 11:25; 12:46; 20:31; Rom. 5:1; 10:9; Phil. 3:9; Heb. 10:38). Wesley stated this truth as follows: "Grace is the source, faith the condition, of salvation" (SSS, I, 38).

Each of the New Testament writers underscores the importance of personal faith as the way to salvation, as did Jesus himself. For instance, John records the following conversation between Jesus and a crowd of people: "They said to him, 'What must we do, to perform the works of God?' Jesus answered them, 'This is the work of God, that you believe in him whom he has sent' " (John 6:28-29). John tells us that he wrote his account of Jesus so that we may believe that Jesus is the Christ and thereby have life in his name (John 20:31). The author of the book of Hebrews tells us that without faith it is impossible to please God (Heb. 11:6). We accept the existence of God through faith; by faith we receive our salvation; by faith we stay strong in our Christian lives. In sum, we are saved by faith (Rom. 10:9; I Pet. 1:5, 9). In recognition of the important place of faith, United Methodism's *Book of Discipline* states, "Through faith in Jesus Christ we are forgiven, reconciled to God, and transformed as people of the new covenant" (*Discipline*, 43).

United Methodists often quote a phrase that appears in Galatians: "faith working through love" (Gal. 5:6). This phrase points to the two sides of faith—*belief* and *action*. The only genuine faith is the faith that is inwardly sincere and demonstrated by deeds (James 2:14-26; see also Matt. 5:16; I Tim. 6:18; Tit. 2:7; James 2:17-18; I Pet. 2:12). Wesley defined faith as "a sure trust and confidence which a man hath in God, that, by the merits of Christ, his sins are forgiven, and he reconciled to the favour of God; whereof doth follow a loving heart, to obey his commandments" (*The Almost Christian*, SSS, I, 63; WJWJ, V, 23). Faith is a necessary work, but not a meritorious work. Our salvation, from beginning to end, rests entirely on grace. God offers us love, pardon, and power, not because we deserve his generosity and good will but because we believe.

Faith does not mean merely an intellectual conviction of the truth of the Christian gospel, as important as such a certitude may be. Our affirming orthodox religious convictions may not necessarily lead us to yield our complete selves to God. John Wesley reminds his readers that faith is not "a speculative, rational thing, a cold, lifeless assent, a train of ideas in the head; but also a disposition of the heart" (*Salvation by Faith*, SSS, I, 40; WJWJ, V, 9). The church in corporate worship sings:

> Faith of our fathers, living still,
> In spite of dungeon, fire, and sword;
> O how our hearts beat high with joy
> Whene'er we hear that glorious word!
> Faith of our fathers, holy faith!
> We will be true to thee till death.
> (Frederick W. Faber; see *UMH*, 710)

Saving faith consists of more than an emotional or warm-hearted experience, as helpful as these feelings may be. Emotions are not always reliable, and they can easily deceive us. Faith may indeed have emotional overtones. But the faith taught by Scripture consists of a sincere conviction of the truth of scriptural Christianity and a decision of the will to depend on Jesus Christ. The essence of saving faith is one's deliberate choice to say yes to the complete reign of God.

Such faith is not a human achievement; it is a gift of God (see Acts 15:11; Rom. 3:24; 5:15; 11:6; Eph. 2:4, 8-9; Tit. 2:11; 3:7). Scripture tells us that we are saved *by* grace, *through* faith (Eph. 2:8-9). Because faith itself is a gift of God's grace, United Methodists prayerfully sing:

> Spirit of faith, come down,
> Reveal the things of God,
> And make to us the Godhead known,
> And witness with the blood.
> 'Tis thine the blood to apply
> And give us eyes to see,
> Who did for every sinner die
> Hath surely died for me.
> (Charles Wesley; see *UMH*, 332)

As a consequence of repentance and faith we are "born from above" to new life in Jesus Christ. The justified person is forgiven, reborn, and called to holiness.

## 2. THE NEW LIFE

Although a rainbow reflects the spectrum of colors, its shades and hues constitute but segments of the single source of light. The single experience of conversion also contains many aspects. The dimensions of Christian experience are not separate experiences, but parts of a whole. The components of the new birth correspond to our basic human needs for forgiveness, acceptance, and divine assistance in our lives. We can analyze conversion this way:

| Human Condition | Human Need | Biblical Solution |
|---|---|---|
| Guilt | Forgiveness | Justification |
| Estrangement | Reconciliation | Adoption |
| Spiritual impotence | New life | Regeneration |
| Spiritual uncertainty | Certitude | Assurance |

In Christian conversion, God forgives our sins (justification), takes us into his family (adoption), and renews us by the Holy Spirit (regeneration). In addition, through the testimony of Scripture and the inner witness of the Holy Spirit, God provides for us the assurance of our salvation.

*(a) Justification.* From the dawn of history humankind has struggled with guilt. Guilt robs us of peace, depresses us, and hinders creative and joyful living. Wrote Felicia Hemans:

There smiles no Paradise on earth so fair
But guilt will raise avenging phantoms there.
(*The Abencerrage*)

An uneasy and guilty conscience constitutes one of humankind's greatest burdens.

People have tried numerous ways to rid themselves of guilt's heavy load. There are those who seek to overcome guilt through elaborate religious rituals. Some have sacrificed their children to a God of fire; some have tried to compensate for their sins with good works; others have inflicted themselves with physical pain. Still others have tried to deny the reality of guilt. But every human effort to remove guilt fails. Only the forgiveness of God can bring the pardon we seek. And divine pardon comes into sharp focus in the biblical doctrine of justification.

*Justification* is a legal term meaning "to acquit" or "to declare not guilty." The Bible often refers to God in judicial terms as the "righteous judge of all the earth" (see Gen. 18:25; Pss. 58:11; 96:13; Eccles. 3:17; Heb. 12:23). In this capacity God exercises judgment against sin (see Ps. 7:11; Isa. 5:16; 10:22; Acts 17:31; Rom. 2:5; 3:5-8). The biblical doctrine of justification means that guilty sinners receive not God's disapproval, but pardon. Justification replaces condemnation. The gospel of grace points to the wonderful truth that the righteous God justifies guilty sinners. Pardoned sinners never cease praising the God of their salvation.

> Amazing grace! How sweet the sound
> That saved a wretch like me!
> I once was lost, but now am found;
> Was blind, but now I see.
> (John Newton; see *UMH*, 378)

The atoning blood of Jesus Christ on the cross constitutes the ground of our pardon (see *Discipline*, 66, 71; BOW, 20).

> He left his Father's throne above
> (So free, so infinite his grace!),

Emptied himself of all but love,
And bled for Adam's helpless race.
(Charles Wesley; see *UMH*, 363)

In establishing the Holy Eucharist, the Lord told his disciples, "This is my blood of the covenant, which is poured out for many for the forgiveness of sins" (Matt. 26:28). We have no forgiveness apart from the shedding of the blood of Jesus Christ and his atoning death on the cross (Acts 20:28; Rom. 5:9-11; Heb. 9:14; I Pet. 1:18-19; I John 1:7; Rev. 1:5; 5:9; 7:14).

John Wesley's sermon *Justification by Faith* has remained a perennial favorite among the people called Methodists. In that sermon Wesley explains, "The plain scriptural notion of justification is pardon, the forgiveness of sins. It is that act of God the Father, whereby, for the sake of the propitiation made by the blood of His Son, He 'showeth forth His righteousness' (or mercy) 'by the remission of the sins that are past' " (SSS, I, 120-21). United Methodism's official doctrinal standards contain similarly clear statements about justification. The Articles of Religion state: "We are accounted righteous before God only for the merit of our Lord and Saviour Jesus Christ, by faith, and not for our own works or deservings" (*Discipline*, 63).

In a similar vein, United Methodism's Confession of Faith declares: "We believe we are never accounted righteous before God through our works or merit, but that penitent sinners are justified or accounted righteous before God only by faith in our Lord Jesus Christ" (*Discipline*, 71). In discussing "Our Doctrinal Heritage," the *Book of Discipline* concludes:

We believe God reaches out to the repentant believer in justifying grace with accepting and pardoning love.

Wesleyan theology stresses that a decisive change in the human heart can and does occur under the prompting of grace and the guidance of the Holy Spirit.

In justification we are, through faith, forgiven our sin and restored to God's favor. . . .

This process of justification and new birth is often referred to as conversion. Such a change may be sudden and dramatic, or gradual and cumulative. It marks a new beginning, yet it is part of an ongoing process. (*Discipline*, 46)

Ⅴ Because we are justified by grace, we can rejoice that God, through Jesus Christ, pardons our sin and proclaims us free from guilt. Charles Wesley rhapsodized:

> Long my imprisoned spirit lay,
> Fast bound in sin and nature's night;
> Thine eye diffused a quickening ray;
> I woke, the dungeon flamed with light;
> My chains fell off, my heart was free,
> I rose, went forth, and followed thee.
> (Charles Wesley; see *UMH*, 363)

Justification by faith stands out as an important dimension of Christian conversion because it frees us from guilt and saves us from God's judgment.

(b) *Adoption*. Before our personal experience of Jesus Christ we do not truly enjoy the privilege of being God's sons and daughters. God is, of course, our Creator. But until we experience saving grace, in the biblical sense God is not our *father*. Indeed, when Jesus talked with certain religious leaders who boasted, "We are not illegitimate children; we have one father, God himself," Jesus plainly told them, "If God were your Father, you would love me. . . . You are from your father the devil, and you choose to do your father's desires"

(John 8:41-42, 44). Scripture teaches us that we all need to be reconciled to God and made members of God's family (II Cor. 5:19-21). Through conversion we become children of God—and God brings us into right relationship with him through *adoption* (Rom. 8:15; II Cor. 6:17-18; Gal. 4:5). When the church expresses its true nature, the sisters and brothers in its community of faith express family love toward one another in attitude, word, and deed (Eph. 2:19).

The theme of adoption appears in the Bible in numerous literary figures of speech. One such figure is that of God who rescues the helpless and becomes their father:

> Father of orphans . . .
>   is God in his holy habitation.
> God gives the desolate a home to live in;
>   he leads out the prisoners to prosperity;
>   but the rebellious live in a parched land.
> (Ps. 68:5-6)

The Old Testament figure of "Father to the fatherless" parallels the New Testament doctrine of adoption.

In our natural state we do not enjoy a proper relationship with God. Sin undermines our fellowship with God, and we need reconciliation (see Ps. 58:3; Jer. 2:5; Ezek. 14:5; Matt. 15:8; Eph. 2:12). Our estrangement from God stems from two sources—our side and God's side. (1) Humankind has rebelled against God and deliberately sinned against him and his will. Paul goes so far as to say that, outside Jesus Christ, we are "enemies" against God (Rom. 5:10) and "strangers to the covenants of promise, having no hope and without God in the world" (Eph. 2:12). (2) The righteous God judges the sin of humankind, as his holiness stands antithetical to evil. Recognizing this truth, the prophet Habakkuk prayed,

"Your eyes are too pure to behold evil, and you cannot look on wrongdoing" (Hab. 1:13; see also Deut. 25:16; II Sam. 11:27; Pss. 5:4; 11:5; Zech. 8:17; Luke 16:15). Reconciliation becomes necessary between two parties when the grounds for fellowship have been violated.

The gospel of grace declares that God (the offended one) took the initiative to reconcile us (the offending ones) and bring us into a right relationship with him. The death of the sinless Savior made possible the reconciliation of the sinning human race. "God proves his love for us in that while we still were sinners Christ died for us. . . . We even boast in God through our Lord Jesus Christ, through whom we have now received reconciliation" (Rom. 5:8, 11). To bring us into his family, God "planned, in his love, that we should be adopted as his own children through Jesus Christ" (Eph. 1:5 JBP). Children of earth become children of heaven:

> Hail the heaven-born Prince of Peace!
> Hail the Sun of Righteousness!
> Light and life to all he brings,
> Risen with healing in his wings.
> Mild he lays his glory by,
> Born that we no more may die,
> Born to raise us from the earth,
> Born to give us second birth.
> (Charles Wesley; see *UMH*, 240)

The experience of conversion restores us to fellowship with God and brings us peace with God (Rom. 5:1; Eph. 2:13, 14; Col. 1:19-22). "To all who received him, who believed in his name, he gave power to become children of God" (John 1:12).

The apostle Paul wrote:

God sent his son . . . in order to redeem those who were under the law, so that we might receive adoption as children. . . . So you are no longer a slave but a child, and if a child then also an heir, through God. (Gal. 4:4-5, 7)

Adoption means that we possess family privileges—we may call God "Abba," or "Father" (see Rom. 8:15; Gal. 4:6). As adopted sons and daughters of God, Christians have access to the Father and a share in the divine inheritance (Rom. 5:2; 8:15-17). This thought shines through Charles Wesley's hymn "Arise, My Soul, Arise":

> My God is reconciled; His pardoning voice I hear;
> He owns me for his child; I can no longer fear:
> With confidence I now draw nigh,
> With confidence I now draw nigh,
> And, "Father, Abba, Father," cry.
> (see *TMH*, 122)

*(c) Regeneration.* Justification and adoption are graces God performs *for* us, and regeneration is a grace that God works *in* us. Regeneration refers to the work of God that imparts spiritual life to those who are "dead in trespasses and sins" (Eph. 2:1; see also Gen. 2:17; Ezek. 18:20; Rom. 6:23; 8:6; James 1:15). According to Paul, unregenerate persons neither glorify God as God nor give thanks to him; their thinking is futile, and their hearts are darkened with spiritual deception (Rom. 1:21). God meets our need for spiritual life through the grace of regeneration. Scripture uses various words to express this change, which God works in us through the Holy Spirit. One such word is *gennao*, which means "to generate," "to beget," or to "give birth to." In regeneration God imparts new life to us. Jesus spoke of this experience as being "born again" or "born from above" (John 3:3). The result of this spiritual birth is a "new creation" in which "everything has become new"

(II Cor. 5:17; see also Gal. 6:15; Eph. 2:15; 4:24; Col. 3:1).

Paul speaks of regeneration in glowing terms. To the Ephesian Christians, he wrote:

> You were dead through the trespasses and sins in which you once lived, following the course of this world, following the ruler of the power of the air, the spirit that is now at work among those who are disobedient. . . . But God, who is rich in mercy, out of the great love with which he loved us even when we were dead through our trespasses, made us alive together with Christ. (Eph. 2:1-2, 4-5; see Col. 2:13)

A similar description of regeneration appears in Titus:

> For we ourselves were once foolish, disobedient, led astray, slaves to various passions and pleasures, passing our days in malice and envy, despicable, hating one another. But when the goodness and loving kindness of God our Savior appeared, he saved us, not because of any works of righteousness that we had done, but according to his mercy, through the water of rebirth [regeneration] and renewal by the Holy Spirit. This Spirit he poured out on us richly through Jesus Christ. (Tit. 3:3-7)

We may describe regeneration as a religious resurrection, the impartation of spiritual vitality and the quickening of new life (COM, 748).

United Methodism's Confession of Faith clearly enunciates the biblical doctrine of regeneration as a work of the Holy Spirit:

> We believe regeneration is the renewal of man in righteousness through Jesus Christ, by the power of the Holy Spirit, whereby we are made partakers of the divine nature and experience newness of life. By this new birth the believer becomes reconciled to God and is enabled to serve him with the will and the affections.

We believe, although we have experienced regeneration, it is possible to depart from grace and fall into sin; and we may even then, by the grace of God, be renewed in righteousness. (*Discipline*, 71; see also p. 46)

The initiative in regeneration is, of course, God's grace, which is based on the work of Christ, effected through the Holy Spirit, and received by faith (John 1:1-3; 3:3-8). Regeneration is a miraculous act of God that imparts life to our sinful spirits, changes our being, and leads to a changed outlook and a new destiny (see SSS, II, 226-43).

### 3. ASSURANCE

Most religions teach that to remain faithful to God we need to live in uncertainty about life after death. These religious systems contend that confidence of our standing with God is neither possible nor desirable. Certitude of salvation allegedly would weaken our moral resolve and undermine good works. The Christian gospel, however, offers us a sure confidence of our reconciliation with God and of our eternal destiny. Scripture teaches us that we do not need to await death to discover whether we are saved or lost.

When a judge pardons an offender, the judge appropriately informs the person of his or her altered standing and new freedom. Similarly, the Bible contains a number of passages telling us that we can *know* that God has pardoned us and has made us members of his family. This certitude of salvation is called "assurance" or "the assurance of faith." Sometimes Scripture refers to the certainty of our standing with God as "the witness of the Spirit," a favorite Wesleyan phrase (Rom. 8:16; Gal. 4:6; I John 5:6).

*(a) The witness of Scripture.* The doctrine of assurance appears again and again in the New Testament (Rom. 8:15-16; II Cor. 6:18; Gal. 4:6; Col. 2:2; I Thess. 1:5;

II Tim. 1:12; I John 2:3; 3:19, 24; 4:13; 5:6, 10). Paul informs us that there is "no condemnation for those who are in Christ Jesus" (Rom. 8:1). Christians have "all the riches of assured understanding" (Col. 2:2) and a "full conviction" of their inheritance in Jesus Christ (I Thess. 1:5). The writer of Hebrews encourages us: "Let us approach [God] with a true heart in full assurance. . . . Let us hold fast to the confession of our hope without wavering, for he who has promised is faithful" (Heb. 10:22-23). Scripture tells believers that they can rest confidently in the knowledge that God will bring to completion the salvation he has begun (II Tim. 1:12; Phil. 1:6).

In Scripture the doctrine of assurance has both objective and subjective grounds. Objectively, assurance is rooted in the authority of God's promises. The declarations of the Bible confirm that, on the basis of the atoning work of Jesus Christ, God justifies, adopts, and regenerates all repentant people who turn to him in faith (see John 3:15; 5:24; 11:25; 12:46; 20:31; Rom. 10:9; II Tim. 3:15; I John 5:1). As the Holy Spirit opens our spiritual understanding, we accept the biblical promises by faith (see *UMH*, 599).

Subjectively, assurance flows from Christian experience. Our inner religious affections bear witness to our awareness of God's love. Christians can have the assurance that they are God's children (Rom. 8:16). Such is the sentiment of the hymn "It Is Well with My Soul" (see *UMH*, 377). Charles Wesley exulted:

We by his Spirit prove and know the things of God,
The things which freely of his love he hath on us bestowed.
(*UMH*, 372)

Interestingly, in Galatians 4:6 we read that it is the Holy Spirit who cries, "*Abba* [Father]," and in Romans 8:15-16 it is the believer who cries, *"Abba."* The Holy Spirit and the human spirit witness *together* to the same truth—we are children of God, free from guilt and alive in Christ. Earlier Methodist hymnals contained this verse by Charles Wesley:

> Holy Ghost, no more delay;
> Come, and in thy temple stay:
> Now thine inward witness bear,
> Strong, and permanent and clear.
> Spring of life, thyself impart;
> Rise eternal in my heart.

The inner testimony of the Spirit remains the *privilege* of every believer. We may pray for this assurance, expect it, and experience it. Our certitude of salvation comes from the action of the Holy Spirit, who works graciously in our lives. The Holy Spirit opens our eyes to truth, transforms us through conversion, and gives us the inner witness that we are Christian believers.

*(b) The testimony of the church.* Although the doctrine of assurance does not belong exclusively to the people called United Methodists, this biblical teaching constitutes "one grand part of the testimony which God has given them" (SSS, II, 343-44). This aspect of the Wesleyan gospel of grace has been responsible, in part, for the drawing power of the Methodist revivals and the earlier growth of the denomination (TPM, 604). Bishop Mack B. Stokes observed: "In no other point did the early Methodists differ so widely from those around them as in insisting upon this experience. It was this which gave life and power to their ministrations. They had personally experienced this gracious state, and were living in its constant enjoyment, and they testified frequently and forcibly of the peace and joy which accompanied it"

(*EWM*, I, 167). The nineteenth-century *Cyclopaedia of Methodism* contended, "A doubting Christian is neither happy nor extensively useful" (COM, 960). The biblical doctrine of Christian assurance speaks to the fundamental desire of persons to know how they stand with God.

Wesley's account of his "Aldersgate experience" has been widely quoted: "I felt my heart strangely warmed. I felt I did trust in Christ, Christ alone for salvation; and an assurance was given me that He had taken away *my* sins, even *mine*, and saved *me* from the law of sin and death" (JJW, I, 476). Wesley later defined the witness of the Spirit as

> an inward impression on the soul, whereby the Spirit of God directly witnesses to my spirit, that I am a child of God; that Jesus Christ hath loved me, and given Himself for me; and that all my sins are blotted out, and I, even I, am reconciled to God. (SSS, I, 207-8)

Philip William Otterbein, one of the founders of the Church of the United Brethren in Christ, and Jacob Albright, the founder of the Evangelical Association, also preached that we can *know* that our sins are forgiven and that we are in union with Jesus Christ:

> To be saved, they held, meant both awareness, as real as any sensory awareness, of God's acceptance and personal commitment to Christ. . . .
>
> . . . Albright and Otterbein . . . stressed conversion, "justification by faith confirmed by a sensible assurance thereof." (*Discipline*, 11, 57)

Concerning the doctrine of assurance, United Methodism's *Book of Discipline* states: "Our Wesleyan theology . . . embraces the scriptural promise that we can expect to receive assurance of our present salvation, as the Spirit 'bears witness with our spirit that we are children of God' " (*Discipline*, 46).

At the 1988 General Conference, The United Methodist Church recognized the *COCU Consensus* as "an expression, in the matters with which it deals, of the Apostolic faith, order, worship, and witness of the Church." That document states, "The Spirit seals God's promise in the hearts of believers" (COCU, 18). Most mainstream Christian denominations hold to a doctrine of assurance, and none have articulated this biblical teaching more helpfully than have the Methodists.

Of course, the danger of self-deception always exists. Some of the most depraved persons in history were convinced that they enjoyed God's special favor and even that their evil deeds advanced God's cause. John Wesley wisely dealt with the fact that the witness of the Holy Spirit can be falsely claimed and asserted. In his opinion, some testimonies to the witness of the Spirit stemmed from "the presumption of a natural mind" or "the delusion of the devil."

It also needs to be said that it is possible to walk away from God and return to our former sins. The Church's Confession of Faith declares, "We believe, although we have experienced regeneration, it is possible to depart from grace and fall into sin; and we may even then, by the grace of God, be renewed in righteousness" (*Discipline*, 71). United Methodism's Articles of Religion state:

> After we have received the Holy Ghost, we may depart from grace given, and fall into sin, and, by the grace of God, rise again and amend our lives. And therefore they are to be condemned who say they can no more sin as long as they live here; or deny the place of forgiveness to such as truly repent. (*Discipline*, 64)

John Wesley insisted that assurance "relates wholly and solely to present pardon, not to future salvation" (WJWJ, IX, 9). Of course, we need not turn away from God's grace. "If we walk in the light as he himself is in the light, we have fellowship with one another, and the blood of Jesus his Son cleanses us from all sin" (I John 1:7).

In Wesleyan theology a good conscience toward God cannot be separated from the lordship of Jesus Christ and the testimony of a transformed life. All claims of possessing the Holy Spirit, apart from confessing Christ as Lord and giving evidence of a changed life, only feed an illusion (John 16:13-15; I Cor. 12:3). The presence of the fruit of the Spirit verifies our position in Christ (see Gal. 5:16-25). John Wesley rightly noted, "We must be holy of heart, and holy in life, before we can be conscious that we are so" (SSS, I, 208).

Through the merits of Jesus Christ, God brings us from darkness to light and from sin to salvation. In God's love, we know pardon, reconciliation, new spiritual life, and the assurance of faith (Eph. 1:3-14). Conversion is a work of God, based on the atonement of Jesus Christ, wrought in us through the person of the Holy Spirit. This experience brings us to the knowledge of God's transforming power, and in this new relationship God calls us to holiness.

# Chapter V

# SANCTIFICATION

*O come and dwell in me, Spirit of power within,*
*And bring the glorious liberty from sorrow, fear, and sin.*
—Charles Wesley

C onversion does not exhaust the possibilities of God's grace, and we should regard Christian conversion not as an end, but as a beginning. Once we are in Christ God begins the process of "renewing the fallen nature and purifying the heart" (COM, 780; see also EWT, 134-35). Scripture contains many passages urging us toward holiness (see Gen. 17:1; Deut. 18:13; I Kings 8:61; Matt. 5:48; 19:21; II Cor. 13:11; Eph. 4:13; Col. 1:28; 3:14; Heb. 6:1; James 1:4; 2:22; 3:2; I John 2:5). This process is called *sanctification* (see EWM, I, 489-91).

Wesleyan theology often uses the phrase "going on to perfection" to refer to sanctification. United Methodism's *Book of Discipline* offers the following statement about Christian perfection.

We hold that the wonder of God's acceptance and pardon does not end God's saving work, which continues to nurture our growth in grace. Through the power of the Holy Spirit we are enabled to increase in the knowledge and love of God and in love for our neighbor.

New birth is the first step in this process of sanctification. Sanctifying grace draws us toward the gift of Christian perfection, which Wesley described as a heart "habitually filled with the love of God and neighbor" and as "having the mind of Christ and walking as he walked."

This gracious gift of God's power and love, the hope and expectation of the faithful, is neither warranted by our efforts nor limited by our frailties. (*Discipline,* 46-47)

The British Methodist pastor William Sangster once said that God can do more for sin than forgive it. God delivers us from both sin's guilt and sin's dominion (Rom. 6:14). United Methodists affirm this truth when they sing:

> He breaks the power of canceled sin,
> He sets the prisoner free;
> His blood can make the foulest clean;
> His blood availed for me.
> (Charles Wesley; see *UMH,* 57)

## 1. SANCTIFICATION IN THE BIBLE

(a) *God's call to holiness.* The subject of holiness constitutes one of the central themes of Scripture. Both the Old Testament and the New Testament carry the message, "As he who called you is holy, be holy yourselves, in all your conduct; for it is written, 'You shall be holy, for I am holy' " (see Lev. 11:45; I Pet. 1:16). Zechariah, the Father of John the Baptizer, spoke a prophecy that Jesus Christ would rescue us so that we "might serve him without fear in holiness and righteousness" all our days (Luke 1:75). The New Testament tells us that Jesus Christ came to make us holy and to save us from our sins (Matt. 1:21; John 17:17-19; Heb. 9:11; 13:11-12). Jesus suffered to "sanctify the people through his own blood" (Heb. 13:12; see John 17:17). Paul stressed that new beings in Christ are "created according to the likeness of God in true righteousness and holiness" (Eph. 4:24). The book of Hebrews even says,

"Pursue . . . holiness without which no one will see the Lord" (Heb. 12:14; see also Lev. 19:2; 20:7; II Cor. 7:1; I Thess. 4:3; 5:23).

When calling Abraham to become the father of a new people, God said, "Walk before me, and be blameless [have no blemishes]" (Gen. 17:1). The Old Testament sacrifices required perfect animals, with no imperfections (see Exod. 12:5; Lev. 22:21; see also Eph 5:27; I Pet. 1:19). The tabernacle priests were to be holy (Exod. 19:22; Lev. 10:3; 21:6; II Chron. 6:41; Isa. 52:11; Mal. 2:7). In establishing the Old Testament covenant, God required perfect obedience (Deut. 18:9-14). And the New Testament allows no compromise in God's standard of holiness: Without holiness we cannot enter God's presence (II Pet. 3:11). In his Sermon on the Mount Jesus taught that holiness involves more than outward performance; it must be established in the heart. With inner righteousness in mind, he insisted, "Be perfect, therefore, as your heavenly Father is perfect" (Matt. 5:48). In Scripture, holiness is not an option; it is a command.

Of course, God alone is absolutely perfect. In recognition of this truth the church sings:

> Only thou art holy; there is none beside thee,
> Perfect in power, in love and purity.
> (Reginald Heber; see *UMH*, 64)

Because God alone is perfect in holiness, only God can make us holy. As stated in United Methodism's *Book of Discipline*, "The restoration of God's image in our lives requires divine grace to renew our fallen nature" (*Discipline*, 46). The end of God's grace is the creation of a holy people, called to "be holy and blameless before him in love" (Eph. 1:4).

*(b) Sanctification as a work of God.* It would be cruel for

103

God to require an imposing standard, and then withhold the necessary assistance from us. The standards of the Sermon on the Mount, for instance, seem unrealistic, except as God empowers us. Holiness would be unattainable without God's grace to do for us what we cannot do for ourselves. King David knew his own heart well enough to know that God alone could make him holy:

> Create in me a clean heart, O God,
> and put a new and right
> spirit within me. (Ps. 51:10)

We are sanctified, not by our efforts, but through God's grace.

The Old Testament contains numerous promises of a day when God would pour out his Spirit of holiness upon the people.

> I will give them one heart, and put a new spirit within them; I will remove the heart of stone from their flesh and give them a heart of flesh, so that they may follow my statutes and keep my ordinances and obey them. Then they shall be my people, and I will be their God. (Ezek. 11:19-20; see also 36:26-27)

The holy God of Israel wants and requires a holy people.

The divine provision for holiness becomes still more evident in the New Testament. Apostolic preaching and teaching centered around two affirmations: (1) Christ's death and Resurrection make our salvation possible and (2) the advent of the Holy Spirit enables us to live holy and righteous lives. Pentecost marked the day of the outpouring of the Holy Spirit, available to "all flesh." God gives us the Holy Spirit, who is "the Spirit of holiness" (Rom. 1:4).

We may define sanctification as the work of God, involving our cooperation, by which God delivers us from the pollution of sin, renewing our nature after the image of God, and enabling us to live self-controlled, upright, and godly lives in this present age (see Titus 2:12). Through the sanctifying work of the Holy Spirit, God indwells his people and imparts his very character into their lives (see Gal. 2:20; Eph. 2:22). Sanctification means that God sets us apart for himself and that we consent to be ruled by God in every area of our lives. Again, we cannot make ourselves holy. Sanctification is the work of God.

*(c) Sanctification and human responsibility.* Wesleyan theology holds the view that the Christian life consists of both a gift and a task. God works, and we respond. This twofold aspect of discipleship is illustrated in the following verse: "Work out your own salvation with fear and trembling; for it is God who is at work in you, enabling you both to will and to work for his good pleasure" (Phil. 2:12-13). Although sanctification is a work of God's grace, we have a part to play in the process. In the Old Testament God calls those whom he has sanctified to sanctify themselves—to separate themselves from all that is unholy and to consecrate their lives completely to God (see Exod. 19:22; Lev. 11:44; Josh. 7:13).

This thought is developed fully in the New Testament, which balances the divine provision with human cooperation. Paul writes:

> We are the temple of the living God; as God said,
> "I will live in them and walk among them,
>     and I will be their God,
>     and they shall be my people.
> Therefore come out from them,
>     and be separate from them,

says the Lord,
and touch nothing unclean;
    then I will welcome you,
and I will be your father,
    and you shall be my sons and daughters,
says the Lord Almighty."

Since we have these promises, beloved, let us cleanse ourselves from every defilement of body and of spirit, making holiness perfect in the fear of God. (II Cor. 6:16–7:1)

The grace of God, as absolutely necessary as it is, becomes effective in our lives in proportion to our response to God's working in our behalf.

Because God gives his grace as we cooperate with him, Scripture speaks of the Christian life as a *walk*—a present, ongoing activity. Our walk with the Lord involves continuing commitment and obedience to him in response to his sanctifying work in our lives.

The biblical teaching on sanctification centers not on perfect performance but on right attitudes and relationships. Specifically, sanctification produces in our lives the qualities of love, joy, peace, patience, kindness, generosity, faithfulness, gentleness, and self-control (Gal. 5:22-23). Jesus summed up the Christian ideal as love for God and love for neighbor (Matt. 5:43-48; 22:36-40). While the implication of this standard seems forbiddingly high, Jesus promised his assistance through the power of the indwelling Holy Spirit. Holiness is not an achievement we must *attain* in our own strength. Rather it is a goal we can *obtain* through grace. The Lord summons us to holiness, and he promises us all the grace that we require (I Thess. 5:23-24).

## 2. THE NEED FOR BALANCE

As with every other Christian doctrine, we understand sanctification only as we turn to Scripture for instruction. The lack of biblical perspective has led to some unbalanced views that, in turn, have spawned pride, confusion, discouragement, defeat, and division. Unfortunately, the doctrine of sanctification has suffered much harm from a failure to consult Scripture. The Christian message of holiness has been damaged both by those who vigorously oppose holiness and by those who zealously champion it. Unfortunately, unbalanced teachings have caused many people to avoid the subject of sanctification.

Yet, the biblical doctrine of sanctification is compellingly attractive, if rightly understood. John Wesley said that the biblical doctrine of sanctification "must be disguised before it can be opposed." His *Plain Account of Christian Perfection* considered the importance of balance:

Q. How shall we avoid setting perfection too high or too low?
A. By keeping to the Bible, and setting it just as high as the Scripture does. It is nothing higher and nothing lower than this. . . . It is love governing the heart and life, running through all our tempers, words, and actions (WJWJ, XI, 397).

*(a) The already and the not yet.* Since the time of the apostolic era, some have contended that the word *perfection* implies a standard impossible to humankind. This objection is understandable because the most mature Christians have flaws in their lives. Yet, we cannot deny that in Scripture God's call to holiness is clear: "God did not call us to impurity but in holiness. Therefore whoever rejects this rejects not human authority but God, who also gives his Holy Spirit to you" (I Thess. 4:7-8). It is not doubletalk to say that sanctification can be described as a *relative perfection.*

John Wesley was familiar with both the ancient Latin

Christian writers and the ancient Greek (or Eastern) writers, and these two traditions understood perfection in different ways—one as absolute, one as relative (see TWS, 72-73). The Latin word *perfectus* means an absolute perfection that is static, one that cannot be improved. Some of Wesley's contemporaries thought of perfection in this Latin sense of absolute perfection, and they quite naturally opposed Wesley when they heard him speak of Christian perfection. Wesley, however, did not understand perfection in this way.

Wesley was influenced by the Christian writers in the Eastern tradition, and that tradition meant something different by the word *perfection*. In contrast to the Latin word *perfectus,* the Greek word *teleiosis* ("perfection") refers to a perfection that is progressive and dynamic. In the Eastern view, perfection means "being perfected." Wesley patiently explained:

> There is no *perfection of degrees,* as it is termed; none which does not admit of a continual increase. So that how much soever any man has attained, or in how high a degree soever he is perfect, he hath still need to 'grow in grace,' and daily to advance in the knowledge and love of God his Savior. (SSS, II, 156)

There is no state of grace that does not allow further growth. John Wesley tirelessly stated that the perfection he advocated was not absolute perfection or sinless perfection—it was *Christian* perfection (see LJW, IV, 213). Paradoxically, it is a perfection that can become more perfect; therefore, Christian perfection is a relative perfection.

In the month of June one might call a small green apple a perfect apple. And in a sense the immature apple is perfect, for in the early summer we cannot reasonably expect the apple to be any more perfectly developed than it is. Yet, the apple is in the process of growing even more perfect, and in the autumn it will have matured. So, in discussing Christian perfection, we can say that it is both *already* and *not yet*. As Charles Wesley wrote:

> Yet when the work is done,
> The work is but begun.

Wesleyan theology distinguishes between purity and maturity. As Wesley so often explained, "Christian perfection . . . does not imply (as some men seem to have imagined) an exemption either from ignorance, or mistake, or infirmities, or temptations" (SSS, II, 156). The EUB *Discipline* carried this helpful comment: "Sanctifying grace does not take away the natural infirmities of [people], yea, it does not even cover them; but on the other hand it sometimes even manifests and exposes them" (EUBD, 53). Whatever sanctification does for us, it moves us toward transparent honesty. Because sanctification does not free us from the human limitations of understanding and judgment, our actions will never reach a perfection that cannot be improved. Our performance remains flawed by our human finitude and handicaps, but our *intentions* can be pure and loving.

(b) *A treasure in earthen vessels.* Paul described the Christian life as consisting of divine and human aspects: "We have this treasure in clay jars, so that it may be made clear that this extraordinary power belongs to God and does not come from us" (II Cor. 4:7). Zealous witnesses to God's sanctifying grace occasionally forget that, for the time being, we remain rooted in this world. Although the Holy Spirit dwells within us, we stay very much human, and our human limitations prevent perfect performance.

Some ancient Eastern teachers carried the biblical teaching about our union with Christ to excess. These writers put forth the notion that through Christian experience we become *deified*. According to the doctrine of deification (sometimes called "apotheosis" or "divinization") we can become so at one with God that we think God's thoughts. To some degree this is true, and such language points to the important truth that God lives within us through the Holy Spirit (see Ezek. 36:27; John 14:17; Rom. 8:9; I Cor. 3:16; I John 2:27). But the concept of divinization goes too far if we claim to have the complete mind of God. Also the doctrine of divinization becomes extreme if it posits the notion that we become so at one with God that we lose our distinct personalities.

We partake of God's holiness much the same as a horseshoe partakes of the heat of a blacksmith's fire. The heat is real in the horseshoe, but the horseshoe remains distinct from the fire. The idea of deification might hypothesize that the horseshoe *becomes* fire. United Methodist theology does not hold to the notion that Christian people become "drops of divinity," which lose their identity in the "ocean of deity" (TWH, 131-34; EUBD, 53).

Wesleyan theology also teaches that sanctification is probationary. We noted earlier that there is no finished state of grace from which one may not "draw back to sin, and finally perish." In his *Journal*, John Wesley noted, "What a grievous error, to think those that are saved from sin cannot lose what they have gained!" (LJW, VI, 32-33). Elsewhere he contended, "There is no such height or strength of holiness as it is impossible to fall from" (WJWJ, XI, 426). Some wag has said, "The United Methodists believe in the doctrine of backsliding, and they practice it!" In spite of that good-natured quip, it does remain important to keep in mind such biblical admonitions as, "Stand firm . . . and do not submit again to a yoke of slavery" (Gal. 5:1; see also John 15:6; I Cor. 10:12).

(c) *A crisis and a process.* For a long time debates have swirled around *when* sanctification occurs. Wesleyan theology teaches that we can benefit from the blessing of sanctification in this life. But is sanctification instantaneous or gradual? The Methodist and the Evangelical United Brethren traditions have urged that sanctification is both—it is immediate and gradual, a crisis and a process.

There is a period of discipline preceding, and a life of growth following, our full sanctification (see JWMT, 93-94). John Wesley stated it this way: "It is often difficult to perceive the instant when a man dies; yet there is an instant in which life ceases. And if ever sin ceases, there must be a last moment of its existence, and a first moment of our deliverance from it" (WJWJ, XI, 442).

On the one hand, too great a stress on the instantaneous aspect of sanctification tends to lead us to trust in *our* work of surrender, faith, and obedience. It can also cause us to consider ourselves as having spiritually "arrived," and we cease growing. Such reasoning could lead to smugness and the neglect of the disciplined use of the means of grace. Paul testified, "I press on toward the goal for the prize of the heavenly call of God in Christ Jesus. Let those of us then who are mature be of the same mind" (Phil. 3:14). The life of holiness is one in which we never cease to grow (WJWJ, VII, 202).

On the other hand, too great a stress on the gradual aspect of sanctification can effectively prevent us from expecting sanctification in the present. The epistles devote a good amount of space to urging us to live holy lives. John Wesley counseled, "Seek and expect it now" (see JWAO, 253).

The EUB *Discipline* gave considerable space to a discussion of sanctification. The following statement about *when* to expect sanctification represents the wisdom distilled from many generations of observation, study, and experience among serious Christians for whom holiness was a consuming passion.

> Experience has moreover taught, that ordinarily this state of Christian perfection is attained gradually, by an upright course of life in following Christ; however, during this gradation, this work is perfected in the soul, sooner or later, by a sudden and powerful influence of grace and outpouring of the Divine Spirit. Those who have actually experienced it, describe this effusion of the Divine life as being similar to the grace of justification, yet far exceeding it. This grace is called Entire Sanctification. (EUBD, 52)

In 1946 the following statement was incorporated into the EUB *Discipline,* and it continues to capture the heartbeat of Methodist theology: "Let us then, seriously and explicitly admonish all believers to strive ardently for Christian Perfection . . . which is accomplished by means of the love of God being perfected in the heart" (EUBD, 54). The 1976 General Conference of The United Methodist Church adopted a report that stated:

> Admittedly, Wesley was a bit unguarded at times when referring to sanctification as an instantaneous experience subsequent to justification. If he were writing today, he would probably place even more emphasis on sanctification as a gradual work of grace characterized by many experiences that keep conversion contemporary. (GCM, 7)

It is likely that, if he were alive today, John Wesley, while not surrendering the belief that we may reach Christian perfection in this lifetime, would confirm that for many people sanctification involves a long process that includes a number of "deeper works of grace."

Christianity is more than an acceptance of a body of beliefs. It is a way of life centered in our union with Jesus Christ and leading to our continuous growth. If Christian perfection seems far from us, we nevertheless may and must move toward it. If the church's mission is to "spread scriptural holiness over these lands," Christians logically must begin with a serious quest for their own personal sanctification.

## 3. SANCTIFICATION IN THE WESLEYAN HERITAGE

*(a) United Methodism's founders.* John Wesley contended that there are three Methodist doctrines that include all the rest—*repentance, faith,* and *holiness* (prevenient grace, converting grace, and sanctifying grace). He wrote, "The first of these we account as it were, the porch of religion; the next, the door; the third, religion itself" (WJWJ, VIII, 472). Wesley's clearest definition of sanctification deserves to be quoted in its entirety because it so faithfully echoes the Bible:

> In one view, it is purity of intention, dedicating all the life to God. It is the giving God all our heart; it is one desire and design ruling all our tempers. It is the devoting, not a part, but all our soul, body, and substance to God. In another view, it is all the mind which was in Christ, enabling us to walk as Christ walked. It is the circumcision of the heart from all filthiness, all inward as well as outward pollution. It is a renewal of the heart in the whole image of God, the full likeness of Him that created it. In yet another, it is the loving God with all our heart, and our neighbour as ourselves. (WJWJ, XI, 444)

As Methodism's founders saw it, the formation of holiness and a Christ-like spirit constitute the heart of biblical religion. They considered this teaching as one of the most important doctrines in the Bible. Wesley once said, "This doctrine [sanctification] is *the grand depositum* which God has lodged with the people called Methodists; and for the sake of propagating this chiefly He appeared to have raised us up" (LJW, VIII, 238). Wesleyan theology views Christian experience as appropriating both the *imputed* righteousness of Christ and the *imparted* righteousness of Christ (SSS, II, 435-36). God imputes righteousness to us in justification and adoption; he imparts righteousness to us in regeneration and sanctification.

The historical sketch of Methodism that appears in the United Methodist *Book of Discipline* underscores the twin biblical focuses on the forgiveness of sin and our deliverance from sin's control:

> [Wesley's] message had a double emphasis, which has remained with Methodism to this day. First was the gospel of God's grace, offered to all and equal to every human need. Second was the moral ideal which this gospel presents. The Bible, he declared, knows no salvation which is not salvation from sin. He called persons to holiness of life, and this holiness, he insisted, is "social holiness," the love and service of others. Methodism meant "Christianity in earnest." . . .
>
> The thrust of the Wesleyan movement and of the United Brethren and Evangelical Association was "to reform the nation, and particularly the Church, and to spread scriptural holiness over the land." . . .
>
> . . . The distinctive shape of the Wesleyan theological heritage can be seen in a constellation of doctrinal emphases that display the creating, redeeming, and sanctifying activity of God. (*Discipline*, 8, 45)

In 1939 when the Methodist Episcopal Church, the Methodist Episcopal Church, South, and the Methodist

Protestant Church united to form the Methodist Church, the following article on sanctification from the Methodist Protestant *Discipline* was placed at the end of the church's Articles of Religion:

> Sanctification is that renewal of our fallen nature by the Holy Ghost, received through faith in Jesus Christ, whose blood of atonement cleanseth from all sin; whereby we are not only delivered from the guilt of sin, but are washed from its pollution, saved from its power, and are enabled, through grace, to love God with all our hearts and to walk in his holy commandments blameless. (*Discipline*, 68)

Along with the Methodist Episcopal Churches and the Methodist Protestant Church, the United Brethren and the Evangelical Association insisted that God has called us to holiness. The *Confession of Faith* carries the following article, "Sanctification and Christian Perfection":

> We believe sanctification is the work of God's grace through the Word and the Spirit, by which those who have been born again are cleansed from sin in their thoughts, words and acts, and are enabled to live in accordance with God's will, and to strive for holiness without which no one will see the Lord.
>
> Entire sanctification is a state of perfect love, righteousness and true holiness which every regenerate believer may obtain by being delivered from the power of sin, by loving God with all the heart, soul, mind and strength, and by loving one's neighbor as one's self. Through faith in Jesus Christ this gracious gift may be received in this life both gradually and instantaneously, and should be sought earnestly by every child of God.
>
> We believe this experience does not deliver us from the infirmities, ignorance, and mistakes common to man, nor from the possibilities of further sin. The Christian must continue on guard against spiritual pride and seek to gain

victory over every temptation to sin. He must respond wholly to the will of God so that sin will lose its power over him; and the world, the flesh, and the devil are put under his feet. Thus he rules over these enemies with watchfulness through the power of the Holy Spirit. (*Discipline*, 72)

Methodism's bishops ask the following questions of those seeking ordination in the church:

1. Have you faith in Christ?
2. Are you going on to perfection?
(*Discipline*, 232)

The goal of Christian perfection was by no means limited to the clergy. John Wesley stated, "It is the peculiar business of Christ to establish the kingdom of heaven in [our] hearts" (ENNT, Matt. 4:17). Concerning sanctification, the *Cyclopaedia of Methodism*, published in 1876 by the Methodist Episcopal Church, said, "A lower standard we could not conceive as coming from God. No less provision could be demanded of his children" (COM, 706). Bishop Francis J. McConnell rightly referred to sanctification as "bringing of all parts of the life under subjection" to Jesus Christ and the laws of his kingdom (*The Essentials of Methodism* [New York: The Methodist Book Concern, 1916], 22).

(*b*) *The contemporary church.* The present liturgy of The United Methodist Church contains prayers for sanctification and the deliverance from sin. The Church at worship petitions for such victory when it prays the Lord's Prayer: "Save us from the time of trial, and deliver us from evil" (*UMH*, 11; see also Matt. 6:13). The Methodist *Book of Worship* (1964) contains this prayer: "O God, who . . . didst send down thy Holy Spirit from above upon thine apostles, and dost evermore send him to renew thine image in our souls: Mercifully grant that by the working of his grace we may be saved from sin and may glorify thee" (BOW, 128).

The church's prayers for freedom from sin include centuries-old prayers of Christians who had a deep heart hunger for purity. For instance, in the Service of Word and Table United Methodists pray:

> Almighty God,
> to you all hearts are open, all desires known,
> and from you no secrets are hidden.
> Cleanse the thoughts of our hearts
> by the inspiration of your Holy Spirit,
> that we may perfectly love you,
> and worthily magnify your holy name,
> through Christ our Lord. (*UMH*, 6)

This prayer speaks of cleansing, perfect love, and worthy living.

*The United Methodist Hymnal* also contains a large section of hymns under the heading "Sanctifying and Perfecting Grace" (382-536). These hymn texts contain a wealth of prayer, instruction, and consolation with respect to God's sanctifying work in Christian believers. In those moments of deepest worship, Christians sincerely join with Charles Wesley in singing this prayer:

> Breathe, O breathe thy loving Spirit
> Into every troubled breast!
> Let us all in thee inherit;
> Let us find that second rest.
> Take away our bent to sinning;
> Alpha and Omega be;
> End of faith, as its beginning,
> Set our hearts at liberty. (see *UMH*, 384)

Opinions of United Methodists sometimes differ on a variety of issues (often the disagreements have to do with emphases and strategies). But all serious Christians in the church agree that God purposes through grace to lift us above the tyranny of sin—and every disciple of Jesus Christ hungers for a pure heart.

(c) *Personal and social holiness.* Scripture balances the interior life of devotion and the outward life of service. John Wesley insisted, "Christianity is essentially a social religion; and . . . to turn it into a solitary one is to destroy it" (SSS, 381-82). He repeatedly declared and demonstrated that there is no holiness but social holiness. Our love for God must necessarily lead to the service of neighbor. The Wesleyan tradition insists that sanctification must lead to good works, and good works cannot be isolated from inner holiness.

In its discussion of the United Methodist doctrinal heritage, *The Book of Discipline* follows a statement on sanctification with a statement on service and good works:

> We insist that personal salvation always involves Christian mission and service to the world. By joining heart and hand we assert that personal religion, evangelical witness, and Christian social action are reciprocal and mutually reinforcing.
>
> Scriptural holiness entails more than personal piety; love of God is always linked with love of neighbor, a passion for justice and renewal in the life of the world.
>
> The General Rules represent one traditional expression of the intrinsic relationship between Christian life and thought as understood within the Wesleyan tradition. Theology is the servant of piety, which in turn is the ground of social conscience and the impetus for social action and global interaction, always in the empowering context of the reign of God. (*Discipline*, 47)

In discussing the General Rules and Social Principles of The United Methodist Church, the *Book of Discipline* states:

We proclaim no *personal gospel* that fails to express itself in relevant social concerns; we proclaim no *social gospel* that does not include the personal transformation of sinners.

It is our conviction that the good news of the Kingdom must judge, redeem, and reform the sinful social structures of our time. (*Discipline*, 49)

Social expressions of Christianity do not *define* Christian faith, they *demonstrate* it. E. Stanley Jones once said something to the effect that religion that does not begin with the individual is not Christian, but neither is religion that stops with the individual. There exists a fundamental distinction between our human efforts to copy the pattern of Jesus' life and God's power at work within us as a consequence of the indwelling Holy Spirit.

In this book we have considered the biblical teaching that God originally created us in his own image and that we exist as unique creatures on the earth (Gen 1:26-27). We also saw that starting with the Fall we forfeited the image of God, fell into sin, and became spiritually bankrupt. But where sin increased, grace abounded all the more, so that, just as sin exercised dominion in death, so also grace exercises dominion through justification, leading to eternal life through Jesus Christ our Lord (Rom. 5:20). The Christian gospel declares that, through the miracle of conversion, God brings us into personal fellowship with himself and begins the process of renewing the image of God within us. These doctrines, then, constitute the gospel of grace.

Each generation faces the same decision that faced Israel centuries ago—the choice between light and darkness, between truth and error, between disintegration and fulfillment. God's message to that ancient nation carried both a warning and a promise: "I call heaven and earth to witness against you today that I have set before you life and death, blessings and curses.

Choose life so that you and your descendants may live, loving the LORD your God, obeying him, and holding fast to him; for that means life to you" (Deut. 30:19-20).

The same choices challenge us today. The gospel of grace speaks the word that God meets us where we are—even in our sins. And God summons us to participate in the wonder of his transforming love in the creation of a new humanity. It is the God who said, "Let light shine out of darkness," who has shone in our hearts to give the light of the knowledge of the glory of God in the face of Jesus Christ (II Cor. 4:6).

# APPENDIXES

## Annotated Bibliography and Keys to Citations and References

**BOR**
*The Book of Resolutions of The United Methodist Church,* Nashville: The United Methodist Publishing House, 1988. *The Book of Resolutions* has been published after each General Conference since 1968. These resolutions pertain to current social issues and concerns. Every four years each new edition contains a cumulative record of the resolutions passed by previous General Conferences, except those resolutions that are no longer timely or that have been rescinded or superseded. When approved by the General Conference, the resolutions state the policies of the Church.

**BOS**
*The Book of Services,* Nashville: The United Methodist Publishing House, 1985. The services in this volume were adopted by the United Methodist General Conference of 1984 to provide "alternatives that more fully reflect . . . developments in the contemporary ecumenical church." *The Book of Services* supplements, but does not replace, the rituals long used by the Methodist and E.U.B. Churches, which appear in *The Book of Discipline.* In 1988 The United Methodist Publishing House released *The Companion to the Book of Services.* This book contains background material and explanations of the services of worship contained in *The Book of Services.*

Borgen, Ole E., *John Wesley on the Sacraments,* Grand Rapids: Zondervan, 1986. This volume constitutes the most definitive study of the Wesleyan theology of the sacraments. Borgen's book also provides an essential basis for our understanding of the nature of worship. The work is scholarly and well documented, while remaining highly readable.

**BOW**
*The Book of Worship for Church and Home,* Nashville: The Methodist Publishing House, 1964. This volume contains the orders of worship,

services for the administration of the sacraments, and aids to worship as used by the former Methodist Church. Much of this material has been incorporated into *The Book of Discipline* and *The United Methodist Hymnal* of The United Methodist Church.

Campbell, Ted, *The Apostolate of United Methodism*, Nashville: Discipleship Resources, 1979. This book demonstrates United Methodism's roots in the apostolic Christian community and United Methodism's broad relationship to ecumenical Christianity. The author shows that faithfulness to Scripture requires an apostolic ministry in the present world.

Chiles, Robert E., *Theological Transition in American Methodism*, Nashville: Abingdon Press, 1965. This study of Methodist theologians traces the evolution of Methodist thought through three major periods in United Methodist history: 1790–1840, Richard Watson and the generation immediately after John Wesley; 1840–1890, John Miley and Methodism in its period of greatest influence; 1890–1935, Albert Knudson and the rise of theological liberalism.

## COCU
*The COCU Consensus: In Quest of a Church of Christ Uniting*, edited by Gerald F. Moede, Baltimore: Approved and commended to the churches by the Sixteenth Plenary of the Consultation on Church Union, 1985. This publication of COCU (Churches of Christ Uniting) outlines the points of agreement among member denominations, of which The United Methodist Church is one. United Methodism's 1988 General Conference recognized this document as an expression of the Apostolic faith.

## COM
Simpson, Matthew, editor, *Cyclopaedia of Methodism*, Philadelphia: Louis H. Everts, 1880 (1876). This volume, long out of print, features concise articles on Methodist Episcopal history, doctrine, and life. The articles represent the consensus of the Church at the time the volume was written. The work went through several revisions and served the Church for many years. The more recent *Encyclopedia of World Methodism* (1974) has replaced this venerable old encyclopedia.

Cushman, Robert, E., *John Wesley's Experimental Divinity*, Nashville: Kingswood Books, 1989. This volume consists of a number of essays centered around American Methodist doctrine in its formative stages (1769–1816). The author insists that the major theological influence on early American Methodism was the work of the Wesleys, and that influence led to early American Methodism's stress on "experimental divinity," or Christian experience.

*Discipline*
*The Book of Discipline of The United Methodist Church*, Nashville: The United Methodist Publishing House, 1988. This volume constitutes United Methodism's official statement regarding the polity and the doctrine of the Church. Although the *Discipline* receives some revision every four years, the doctrinal standards remain fixed. Of particular doctrinal significance are The Articles of Religion of the Methodist Church, The Confession of Faith of the Evangelical United Brethren Church, and The General Rules.

Eller, Paul Himmel, *These Evangelical United Brethren*, Dayton: The Otterbein Press, 1950. This book serves as an introduction to the Evangelical United Brethren Church. In addition to dealing with historical material, the author presents the basic theological issues that have been important to the EUB tradition.

ENNT
Wesley, John, *Explanatory Notes Upon the New Testament*, Grand Rapids: Baker Book House, 1982. Along with John Wesley's standard sermons and the Articles of Religion, this work constitutes part of the doctrinal standards of United Methodism.

EUBD
*The Discipline of the Evangelical United Brethren Church*, Dayton, OH, and Harrisburg, PA: The Otterbein Press and the Evangelical Press, 1947 edition. This edition is the first version of the *Discipline* of the newly merged Evangelical United Brethren Church, which came into being in 1946. This volume contains the official historical and doctrinal statements of this denomination, which merged with the Methodist Church in 1968 to become The United Methodist Church.

EWM
Harmon, Nolan B., ed., *The Encyclopedia of World Methodism*, 2 vols., Nashville: The United Methodist Publishing House, 1974. This important work provides basic information regarding the history, doctrines, institutions, and persons of world Methodism. This reference set was sponsored by the World Methodist Council and the Commission on Archives and History of The United Methodist Church. The work serves the church as the successor of Matthew Simpson's *Cyclopaedia of Methodism*, 1876.

EWT
Mickey, Paul A., *Essentials of Wesleyan Theology*, Grand Rapids: Zondervan, 1980. This book outlines and expands the basic Wesleyan theological motifs that appear in United Methodism's Articles of Religion, John Wesley's *Journal*, his *Explanatory Notes Upon the New Testament*, and his *Sermons*. The study is written in the context of the

Junaluska Affirmation, which was formulated in 1975. The book reflects an orthodox theological framework and an irenic spirit.

## GCM
*Guidelines for The United Methodist Church and the Charismatic Movement,* Nashville: Discipleship Resources, 1976. This document was adopted at the 1976 General Conference during the rise of the Charismatic movement within United Methodism, and this statement serves as the Church's official statement regarding this subject. This document contains balance, good judgment, and helpful theological reflection in its brief number of pages.

## GFH
*Grace, Faith, and Holiness: A Wesleyan Systematic Theology,* Kansas City: Beacon Hill Press, 1988. This one-volume systematic theology quotes generously from John Wesley and from theologians in the Wesleyan tradition. Students of John Wesley will recognize that the title of Dunning's book echoes Wesley's paradigm of Christian experience—prevenient grace, converting grace, and sanctifying grace.

Harper, Steve, *Devotional Life in the Wesleyan Tradition,* Nashville: The Upper Room, 1983. This book focuses on spiritual formation and growth in Christian discipleship. As an outline for the work, the author uses the Wesleyan paradigms of the instituted and prudential means of grace.

Heidinger, James V., ed., *Basic United Methodist Beliefs,* Wilmore, KY: Good News Books, 1986. This volume's articles are predicated on the thesis that the 1972 General Conference adoption of "theological pluralism" failed to provide adequate doctrinal guidelines and boundaries for the Church. The book's thirteen chapters deal with basic theological issues, and they are written by a United Methodist bishop, a seminary president, an editor, and prominent United Methodist professors and pastors. A handy collection of theological reflections in the classical orthodox tradition.

## JJW
Curnock, Nehemiah, ed. *The Journal of John Wesley,* 8 vols., London: Epworth, 1938. These volumes have long served as the standard edition of John Wesley's journal. This set also contains Curnock's transcription of John Wesley's unpublished diaries. In time, the Bicentennial Edition of the Works of John Wesley (vols. 21-24) will become the standard edition of John Wesley's journal and diaries.

## JWAO
Outler, Albert, ed., *John Wesley,* New York: Oxford University Press, 1964. This volume contains a selection of John Wesley's most

representative theological writings grouped under selected headings. Outler provides historical introductions and critical evaluations of Wesley's thought in relationship to the broader context of Christian thought.

JWMT
Harper, Steve, *John Wesley's Message for Today*, Grand Rapids: Zondervan, 1983. From a Wesleyan perspective, this book deals with the fundamental components of Christian experience. The author shows how John Wesley made "the religion of the heart" come alive to his generation, and Harper applies these insights to our time. This work combines solid theological thinking with a readable style and pastoral wisdom.

JWTT
Williams, Colin W., *John Wesley's Theology Today*, Nashville: Abingdon Press, 1983. This monograph discusses the main beliefs of John Wesley, with a special focus on Christian experience. Williams's work carries on a running comparison of Wesley with other theological traditions, including the Protestant reformers and Roman Catholicism.

LJW
Telford, John, ed. *The Letters of John Wesley*, 8 vols., London: Epworth, 1964. This edition serves as the standard collection of John Wesley's correspondence. The Bicentennial Edition of the Works of John Wesley (vols. 25-31), when completed, will become the standard edition of the letters of John Wesley. Frank Baker has already completed volumes 25 and 26.

McCutcheon, William J., "American Methodist Thought and Theology, 1919-1960," *The History of American Methodism*, ed. Emory Stevens Bucke, 3 vols., New York and Nashville: Abingdon Press, 1964, III, 261-327. This article on American Methodism considers theological liberalism, popular piety, "neo-Wesleyanism," and social issues in Methodism. The author also sketches the divergent theological ideas of selected Methodist theologians.

Oden, Thomas C., *Doctrinal Standards in the Wesleyan Tradition*, Grand Rapids: Francis Asbury Press, 1988. This book is "required reading" for those who wish to understand the roots of the Wesleyan tradition. The author addresses the issue of doctrinal pluralism and discusses the sources of authority for current United Methodism. The work is impressively researched, and it meets a basic need in the Church.

O'Malley, J. Steven, *Pilgrimage of Faith: The Legacy of the Otterbeins*, Metuchen, NJ: The Scarecrow Press, 1973. This book explores the

European backgrounds of the United Brethren tradition. The author shows how the theology of the Otterbein brothers influenced Christianity in America. Two Otterbein brothers—Georg Gottfried and Johann Daniel—ministered in Europe. Philip Wilhelm (William) Otterbein, of course, came to America and founded the Church of the United Brethren in Christ.

Outler, Albert C., *Evangelism in the Wesleyan Spirit*, Nashville: Tidings, 1971. This book was written by one of United Methodism's foremost authorities on John Wesley's thought. The work is penetrating, yet not overly burdened with detail. Outler examines John Wesley as an evangelist, then he considers the content of Wesley's message and the implications for Wesleyan evangelism in our time.

PDL

Langford, Thomas A., *Practical Divinity: Theology in the Wesleyan Tradition*, Nashville: Abingdon Press, 1983. This book surveys theology in the Wesleyan tradition as it appears in British and American Methodism as well as in black Methodist churches and the holiness branches of Methodism. Langford shows the continuing vitality of Methodist thought in the context of the ecumenical Christian community.

Peters, John Leland, *Christian Perfection and American Methodism*, Grand Rapids: Zondervan, 1985. This book demonstrates that John Wesley's teaching on the doctrine of Christian perfection is rooted in Scripture and the teachings of the ancient church. This study shows how the doctrine of Christian perfection was transplanted, developed, and modified in American Methodism.

PJCW

Osborn, G., ed. *The Poetical Works of John and Charles Wesley*, 13 vols., London: Wesleyan Methodist Conference Office, 1868–1872. This definitive multivolume set serves as the standard collection of the hymns and poetry written by the Wesleys.

PWO

Arthur C. Core, ed., *Philip William Otterbein: Pastor, Ecumenist.* Dayton, OH: The Board of Publication, The Evangelical United Brethren Church, 1968. The first section of this volume contains essays about Otterbein written by Arthur C. Core, William J. Hinke, Raymond W. Albright, and Paul H. Eller. Part two contains sermons and letters of Otterbein, along with several important United Brethren documents of historical significance.

Sangster, William E., *The Path to Perfection*, London: The Epworth Press, 1957 (1943). Sangster's study of sanctification is at the same time scholarly and readable. This carefully balanced statement combines Scripture, John Wesley's teaching, and contemporary applications of the idea of Christian perfection.

Smith, Timothy, *The Pentecost Hymns of John and Charles Wesley*, Kansas City, MO: Beacon Hill Press, 1982. This collection of Pentecost hymns of the Wesleys contains an introduction and commentary. This inexpensive book will be of interest to those who wish to study some of the Wesleyan hymns that do not appear in the present United Methodist hymnal.

SSS
Sugden, E. H., ed. *The Standard Sermons of John Wesley*, 2 vols., London: Epworth, 1956. At one time this set was the most frequently used edition of John Wesley's sermons. In the footnoting apparatus Sugden provides numerous annotations that help the reader to understand better these sermons, which constitute part of the doctrinal standards for United Methodism.

Stokes, Mack B., *Major United Methodist Beliefs*, rev. ed., Nashville: Abingdon Press, 1989. This book, written by a United Methodist bishop, has been revised several times. It continues to serve the Church as an introductory text to United Methodist teaching, with a practical focus on Christian experience. This edition takes into account the Evangelical United Brethren traditions, while emphasizing the towering figure of John Wesley.

Stokes, Mack B., *Our Methodist Heritage*, Nashville: The Graded Press, 1963. This book begins with the home and family experiences of Susanna and Samuel Wesley, parents of Methodism's founder. Bishop Stokes traces John Wesley's development as a Christian and as a thinker, showing the practical and theological genius of Methodism's founder.

TJW
Cannon, William Ragsdale, *The Theology of John Wesley With Special Reference to the Doctrine of Justification*, New York, Nashville: Abingdon Press, 1946. This work is especially helpful in giving perspective regarding John Wesley's place in the history of Christian thought. The author summarizes other theological viewpoints and compares them to those of Wesley. This scholarly work is considered by many to be one of the best studies of John Wesley's theology.

TMH
*The Methodist Hymnal*, Nashville: The Methodist Publishing House, 1964. This older hymnal contains a number of the hymns of Charles

Wesley that do not appear in the current United Methodist hymnal. Several of these Wesleyan hymns have been cited in this book.

TPM

McCulloh, Gerald O., and Timothy L. Smith, "The Theology and Practices of Methodism, 1876-1919," *The History of American Methodism*, ed. Emory Stevens Bucke, 3 vols., New York and Nashville: Abingdon Press, 1964, II, 592-659. These pages deal with Christian experience and theological reflection in the Methodist Episcopal Church during the late nineteenth and early twentieth centuries in America.

TRTN

Hynson, Leon O., *To Reform the Nation: Theological Foundations of Wesley's Ethics*, Grand Rapids: Francis Asbury Press, 1984. This book analyzes the theological roots of the reforming impulses of the Wesleyan movement. The study treats John Wesley's understanding of the biblical basis for ethics, and Hynson gives especially helpful attention to the biblical and Wesleyan doctrine of creation.

TWH

Lawson, John, *The Wesley Hymns as a Guide to Scriptural Teaching*, Grand Rapids: Zondervan, 1988. This book arranges the texts of a number of Wesley hymns according to theological themes and in the righthand margin lists the Scripture references that inspired the lines of the verses. Serious students of Scripture and ordinary Christians will be amazed at the ingenious way the Wesley's used the Bible—always with integrity.

TWS

Outler, Albert, *Theology in the Wesleyan Spirit*, Nashville: Tidings, 1975. This volume is a sequel to the author's *Evangelism in the Wesleyan Spirit*. In a delightfully elegant style, Outler unfolds John Wesley's theological method, his view of original sin, his understanding of the gospel, and the Wesleyan distinctive of holiness.

Tyson, John, ed., *Charles Wesley: A Reader*, New York: Oxford University Press, 1989. This volume contains important selections from Charles Wesley's hymns, poetry, letters, and sermons. The editor's introduction and commentary yield valuable insights regarding the theology and influence of Charles Wesley.

UMH

*The United Methodist Hymnal: Book of United Methodist Worship*, Nashville: The United Methodist Publishing House, 1989. Long in the planning and development stage, this hymnal seeks theological balance, cultural diversity, and congregational usefulness. Due to the careful consultative process, this collection is "a people's hymnal." Two helpful companion volumes to *The United Methodist Hymnal* have been released by The United Methodist Publishing House: *The Hymns of the United Methodist Hymnal*, ed. Diana Sanchez, 1989; and *The Worship Resources of the United Methodist Hymnal: Introduction to the General Services, Psalter, and Other Acts of Worship*, ed. Hoyt L. Hickman, 1989. Both volumes contain helpful information and useful bibliographies.

Watson, Philip S., *The Message of the Wesleys*, Grand Rapids: Francis Asbury Press, 1984. This book combines a brilliant introduction and running commentary with representative selections from the Wesleys. The author stresses instruction and devotion as necessary corollaries.

Wesley, John, ed., *A Christian Library*, 30 vols., London: printed by T. Cordeaux for T. Blanshard, 1819. These volumes provide helpful background reading regarding the ideas that helped to shape Wesleyan theology. John Wesley promoted this collection as "Extracts from and Abridgements of the Choicest Pieces of Practical Divinity Which Have Been Published in the English Tongue." The set was of special usefulness to the early Methodist preachers.

WJW
Baker, Frank, textual ed., and Richard P. Heitzenrater, gen. ed. *The Works of John Wesley*, Nashville: Abingdon Press, 35 vols. (planned). This edition, begun by Oxford University Press, will be completed by Abingdon Press. When all the volumes have been published, this set of Wesley's works will serve as the definitive edition of John Wesley's writings. The volumes are appearing one at time, and a number have already been published.

WJWJ
Jackson, Thomas, ed. *The Works of John Wesley, A.M., Sometime Fellow of Lincoln College, Oxford, with the Last Corrections of the Author*, 14 vols., London: Wesleyan-Methodist Book Room, 1831; exact reprint available from Grand Rapids: Baker Book House, 1978. Long considered the standard edition of John Wesley's works, the Jackson edition will continue to serve until the Abingdon Press edition is completed under the editorship of Richard P. Heitzenrater and Frank Baker.

WOS
Collins, Kenneth J., *Wesley on Salvation*, Grand Rapids: Francis Asbury Press, 1989. This monograph, based on the standard fifty-three sermons of John Wesley, traces the order of salvation as taught by Methodism's founder. The book is documented, balanced, and well written.

# Key Scripture References

## I. CREATION

Gen. 1:1-31; 2:1-7; 5:1-3; 9:6; Exod. 4:11; 20:1-6, 11-13; Deut. 4:9, 32; 6:7; 32:6, 15, 18; I Sam. 2:8; II Kings 19:15; I Chron. 16:26; Neh. 9:6; Job 9:8-9; 10:8-9, 11-12; 12:9-10; 10:3, 8; 12:7-9; 26:7, 13; 27:3; 28:23-26; 31:15; 33:4; 34:19; 37:16, 18; 38:4-13, 36; Pss. 8:3, 5-8; 19:1-6; 24:1-2; 33:6-9, 15; 65:6, 13; 69:34; 74:16-17; 78:69; 86:9; 89:11-12, 47; 90:2; 94:9; 95:4-6; 97:6; 98:8; 100:3; 102:25; 103:22; 104:1-25, 30; 119:73, 90-91; 21:2; 124:8; 135:5-9; 139:13; 146:5-6; 149:2; Prov. 3:19-20; 8:22-31; 16:4; 20:12; 22:2; 26:10; 30:4; Eccles. 3:11; 7:29; 11:5; 12:1; Isa. 17:7; 37:16; 40:12, 26-28; 42:5; 43:1, 7, 15; 44:2, 23-24; 45:7, 12, 18; 48:13, 16; 51:13; 64:8; 65:17; 66:2; Jer. 5:22; 10:12-13, 16; 17:9; 27:5; 31:35; 32:17; 33:2; 51:15-16, 19; Dan. 5:23; Amos 4:13; 5:8; 9:6; Jonah 1:9; Zech. 12:1; Mal. 2:10; Matt. 5:22; 16:26; 25:34; Mark 10:6; 13:19; John 1:3, 10; Acts 4:24; 7:49-50; 14:15-17; 17:22-29; Rom. 1:20-23; 3:13; 4:17; 11:36; I Cor. 8:6; 12:8, 24; 15:38; II Cor. 4:6; 5:5; Eph. 3:9; 6:4; Col. 1:16-17; I Tim. 6:13; Tit. 2:4; Heb. 1:1-3; 2:10; 3:4; 11:3; 12:9; James 3:9; I Pet. 4:19; I John 3:15; Rev. 3:14; 4:11; 10:6; 14:7.

## II. SIN

Gen. 3:1-13, 19; 6:5-7, 12; 39:9; Exod. 20:5; 23:33; 32:21, 31, 34; 34:7-8; Num. 14:18; Deut. 24:16; 25:16; 31:17-18; Josh. 7:12; I Kings 8:46; 11:9; 14:22; I Chron. 10:13; II Chron. 7:14; 24:20; Job 14:4; 15:16; Pss. 4:4; 5:4-6; 10:3; 11:5; 14:3; 25:11; 32:5; 34:21; 38:18; 39:11; 51:2-5; 52:3; 53:3; 66:18; 69:5; 95:10; 106:6, 43; 119:11, 133, 176; 130:3; 140:11; Prov. 2:14; 5:22; 6:14; 8:36; 10:19; 11:3, 19; 14:34; 15:8-9, 26; 20:9; 21:27; 24:8-9; 29:6, 16; Eccles. 7:20; 8:7; 9:3; Isa. 1:5-6, 16, 18; 3:9; 6:5; 53:4-6; 55:7; 59:1-2, 12-15; 64:5-7; Jer. 3:21-22, 25; 6:17-18; 7:24; 14:10; 17:9; 30:12; 44:4, 21-22; Ezek. 18:4; 20:16; Hos. 13:9; Mic. 3:4, 6:7, 18; 7:2; Hab. 1:13;

Zech. 8:17; Matt. 5:28; 8:17; 9:13; 12:35; 13:41; 15:8-20; 18:6; 23:13-29; Luke 13:27; 16:15; 18:9; John 5:14; 8:7, 11, 34; 15:22; 16:8-9; Rom. 1:18–3:19, 23; 2:12; 3:21-26; 5:6, 12-21; 6:12, 16, 20, 23; 7:11, 14, 17, 20, 23; 8:5-8; 14:23; Gal. 1:4; I Cor. 5:6; 15:3, 34; II Cor. 5:15; Gal. 1:4; 3:22; 5:19-21; Eph. 2:1-3, 8-9; 4:22; II Thess. 2:11-12; Tit. 2:14; 3:3; Heb. 2:3; 3:13; 12:1; 12:15; James 1:14-15; 2:10-11; 4:1-3, 17; I Pet. 2:24; I John 1:8, 10; 2:1; 3:4-10, 15; 5:17, 19; Rev. 1:5-6; 5:9.

## III. GRACE

Gen. 6:8; 18:26; 46:4; Exod. 3:12; 20:24; 32:26; 33:17; Lev. 26:11-12; Num. 14:14; 23:20-21; Deut. 7:6-9; 30:14-20; 33:23; Josh. 1:5, 9; 24:15; I Kings 6:13; II Chron. 15:2; 18:21; Job 10:12; 22:27; 29:3-5; Psalm 3:8; 5:12; 18:19, 25; 25:14; 30:7; 36:9; 37:18, 23; 44:3; 46:7; 48:9-10; 59:10; 84:11; 89:17; 92:19; 94:17-19; 102:13; 115:12-13; 138:3; 143:11; 147:11; 149:4; Prov. 3:4, 24, 32, 35; 4:18; 10:6, 22, 24; 11:27; 12:2; 14:9; 16:7; Isa. 26:10; 28:5; 30:26; 33:21; 41:10; 43:21; 45:22; 54:8; 55:1; 60:10; Jer. 1:5; 15:20; 31:3; Lam. 3:24; Ezek. 37:27; 39:29; 48:35; Dan. 9:18; 10:18-19; Hos. 14:4; Joel 2:27; 3:16-17; Jonah 2:8; Hag. 1:13; Zech. 2:5; 9:16; 12:10; Matt. 22:9; 25:31-33; Mark 10:21; Luke 1:28, 30, 66; John 1:1-17; 3:16-17; 7:37; 6:44-45; 14:16-17, 19-21, 23; 15:15; Acts 4:33; 6:8; 10:35; 11:23; 13:43; 15:11; 18:27; 20:24, 32; 26:22; Rom. 2:4, 29; 3:22-24; 4:4-5, 16; 5:2, 8-21; 15, 17, 20-21; 6:14-15; 8:30; 9:14-16; 10:12; 11:5-6; 12:6; I Cor. 1:3-4, 9; 2:9-16; 3:10, 21-23; 10:13; 15:10; 16:23; II Cor. 1:2, 12; 4:15; 6:1; 8:1, 9; 9:8, 14; 10:18; 12:9; 13:14; Gal. 1:3, 15-16; 2:21; 4:6; 5:4; 6:18; Eph. 1:2-3, 6-7; 2:4-9, 13-14, 18, 22; 3:12-13; 4:7; 5:2; Phil. 1:2, 6-11; 2:13; Col. 1:2, 11; 4:6, 18; I Thess. 1:1; 3:12-13; 5:28; II Thess. 1:2-3, 12; 2:16; 3:18; I Tim. 1:2, 14; 2:4; 6:21; II Tim. 1:2, 9; 2:1; 4:22; Tit. 1:4; 2:11; 3:7, 15; Philm. 1:25; Heb. 4:16; 10:19, 22, 29; 11:5; 12:15; 13:9, 25; James 4:6; I Pet. 1:2-3, 5, 10, 13; 2:9; 4:10; 5:5, 10, 12; II Pet. 1:2; 3:18; I John 3:19; 4:17-18; II John 1:3; Jude 1:4, 24, 25; Rev. 1:4-6; 3:10, 20; 21:3; 22:17, 21.

## IV. CONVERSION

Gen. 2:17; Deut. 30:6, 10; I Kings 8:58; II Kings 17:13; II Chron. 7:14; Pss. 22:27; 25:11; 34:14; 36:9; 37:27; 40:3; 51:2, 7-13; 65:3; 79:9; 110:3; Prov. 14:27; Isa. 1:18, 25; 4:4; 12:3; 26:12; 32:17; 35:5-6; 40:31; 42:16; 44:3-5; 53:11; 55:1-3, 7; 56:5; 59:20; 62:2; Jer. 13:23; 15:19; 17:14; 18:11; 24:7; 31:33, 34; 32:38-40; 33:6, 8; 35:15; 36:3, 7; Ezek. 11:19-20; 14:6; 18:20, 23, 30-32; 33:11; 36:25-26; 37:4-14; Zech. 3:4; 12:10; 13:1; Mal. 3:3; Matt. 3:2; 4:17; 6:14-15; 9:6; 11:20; 12:23; 18:3; 26:28; Mark 1:15; 2:10; 6:12; Luke 1:16-17; 5:24; 8:35-39; 13:3, 5; 15:7; John 1:4, 12-13; 3:3, 6-7, 15; 4:10, 14; 5:24; 6:51, 57; 8:12, 36; 10:9-10; 11:25; 12:46; 20:31; Acts 2:38, 47; 3:19, 26; 8:22; 11:21; 13:39; 14:15; 15:9; 17:30; 20:28; 26:18; Rom. 1:12; 2:28-29; 3:20, 22, 28; 5:1-2, 9-11; 6:3-23; 7:6; 8:2-16, 23; 9:4, 30; 10:9, 17; 12:2; 15:16; I Cor. 1:9, 24, 30; 2:12, 14-16 6:11; 12:13; 15:10;

II Cor. 1:21-22; 3:3, 18; 4:6, 16; 5:5, 17; 6:17-18; Gal. 2:16, 20; 3:8, 11, 22-26; 4:5-6; 6:15; Eph. 1:5; 2:1, 5-9, 15, 19; 3:17; 4:24; 6:16; Phil. 3:9; Col. 1:19-22; 2:11-13; 3:1, 9-10; 1:23; II Thess. 1:4; I Tim. 1:14, 19; 3:9, 13; 6:11-12; II Tim. 3:15; Tit. 3:5-6; Heb. 4:1-11, 14; 9:14; 10:22, 38; 11:6; 13:7; James 1:3, 15, 18; I Pet. 1:3, 18-19, 22-23; II Pet. 1:3, 4; I John 1:7, 9, 14; 3:1; 4:7; 5:1, 4-5, 11-12, 18; Rev. 1:5; 2:5, 16, 21; 3:3, 12, 19; 5:9; 7:14; 15:3; 21:7.

# V. SANCTIFICATION

Gen. 17:1; Deut. 18:13; Exod. 12:5; 19:22; Lev. 11:45; 19:2; 20:26; 22:21; Num. 11:18; Josh. 3:5; I Sam. 16:5; I Kings 8:61; II Chron. 6:41; 29:6; Job 36:7; Pss. 24:3, 4; 32:2; 34:15; 51:2, 7; 92:12; Isa. 1:16, 18; 3:10; 52:11; Jer. 4:14; Ezek. 36:25; 37:28; Hos. 10:12; Zech. 3:4; 13:1; Mal. 2:7; 3:3; Matt. 5:8, 20, 48; 13:43; Luke 1:74-75; John 15:6; 17:17, 19; Acts 20:32; 26:17; I Cor. 1:2, 30; 6:11; 10:12; 14:20; 15:34; II Cor. 7:1; 9:10; 13:11; Gal. 2:20; 5:1; Eph. 3:19; 4:13, 15, 22-24; 5:25-27; 6:14; Phil. 1:6, 11; 2:15; Col. 1:28; I Thess. 3:12; 4:3; 5:23; II Thess. 2:13; I Tim. 1:5; 5:22; II Tim. 2:21; Heb. 2:11; 6:1; 9:14; 10:16; 13:12; 12:14; James 1:4, 27; 4:8; I Pet. 1:2, 16, 19, 22; 2:9; II Pet. 1:5-6; 3:11, 14; I John 1:7; 2:14; 3:3; Jude 1:1; Rev. 7:14; 14:4-5.

# Relevant United Methodist Documents and Hymns

Unless otherwise noted, the hymns and poems appear in *The United Methodist Hymnal*, 1989. Hymns designated with the code *TMH* can be found in *The Methodist Hymnal*, 1964.

## I. CREATION

*The Book of Discipline:* pages 42-44, 96

### Hymns

All Beautiful the March of Days, *TMH*, 33
All Creatures of Our God and King, 62; *TMH*, 60
All Things Bright and Beautiful, 147; *TMH*, 34
For the Beauty of the Earth, 92; *TMH* 35
God Created Heaven and Earth, 151
God of the Earth, the Sky, the Sea, *TMH*, 36
God, Who Stretched the Spangled Heavens, 150
Hark! the Herald Angels Sing, 240; *TMH*, 387
I Sing the Almighty Power of God, 152; *TMH*, 37
Joyful, Joyful, We Adore Thee, 89; *TMH*, 38
O How Glorious, Full of Wonder, *TMH*, 41
O Lord, Our Lord, in All the Earth, *TMH*, 44
Praise to the Lord, the Almighty, 139; *TMH*, 55
Sing to the Great Jehovah's Praise, *TMH*, 510
The Spacious Firmament of High, *TMH*, 43
This Is My Father's World, 144; *TMH*, 45
To Bless the Earth, God Sendeth, *TMH*, 512

## II. SIN

*The Book of Discipline:* pages 42, 62-63, 67, 71-72

## Hymns

Ash Wednesday, 353
Come, Ye Sinners, Poor and Needy, 340; *TMH*, 104
Creator of the Earth and Skies, 450
Dear Lord and Father of Mankind, 358; *TMH*, 235
Depth of Mercy, 355
I Am Coming to the Cross, *TMH*, 116
I Heard the Voice of Jesus Say, *TMH*, 117
I Surrender All, 354
Jesus, the Sinner's Friend, to Thee, *TMH*, 118
Just as I Am, Without One Plea, 357; *TMH*, 119
Nothing but the Blood, 362
Pass Me Not, O Gentle Savior, 351; *TMH*, 145
Rock of Ages, Cleft for Me, 361; *TMH*, 120
Sinners, Turn: Why Will You Die, 346

# III. GRACE

*The Book of Discipline:* pages 17, 43, 46, 48, 63, 68, 72, 74-77

## Hymns

Alas! and Did My Savior Bleed, 359; *TMH*, 415
Amazing Grace, 378, *TMH*, 92
And Can It Be that I Should Gain, 363; *TMH*, 527
Come, All of You, 350
Come, Sinners, to the Gospel Feast, 339; *TMH*, 102
Freedom in Christ, 360
Grace Greater than Our Sin, 365
How Happy Every Child of Grace, *TMH*, 115
I Sought the Lord, 341; *TMH*, 96
Jesus, Lover of My Soul, 479; *TMH*, 126
Let All on Earth Their Voices Raise, *TMH*, 39
Nothing but the Blood, 362
Where Shall My Wondering Soul Begin, 342

# IV. CONVERSION

*The Book of Discipline:* pages 11, 42-43, 46, 57, 63, 66, 71

## Hymns

An Invitation to Christ, 466
Arise, My Soul, Arise, *TMH*, 122
Blow Ye the Trumpet, Blow, 379; *TMH*, 100

Break Thou the Bread of Life, 599, *TMH*, 369
Come, Ye Disconsolate, 510; *TMH*, 103
Forgive Our Sins as We Forgive, 390
How Can We Sinners Know, 372; *TMH*, 114
I Stand Amazed in the Presence, 371
It Is Well with My Soul, 377
Let Us Plead for Faith Alone, 385,
O Happy Day, That Fixed My Choice, 391; *TMH*, 128
Rock of Ages, Cleft for Me, 361; *TMH*, 120
Standing on the Promises, 374; *TMH*, 221

# V. SANCTIFICATION

*The Book of Discipline:* pages 8, 45-47, 49, 68, 72, 232

## *Hymns*

Breathe on Me, Breath of God, 420; *TMH*, 133
Close to Thee, 407; *TMH*, 176
Come, O Thou Traveler Unknown, 387
For Holiness of Heart, 401
For Illumination, 477
For Our Country, 429
For True Life, 403
Have Thine Own Way, Lord, 382; *TMH*, 154
Holy Spirit, Truth Divine, 465; *TMH*, 135
How Can We Sinners Know, 372; *TMH*, 114
I Need Thee Every Hour, 397
I Want a Principle Within, 410; *TMH*, 280
It Is Well with My Soul, 377
Jesus Calls Us, 398; *TMH*, 107
Jesus, Lover of My Soul, 479; *TMH*, 125
Jesus, Thine All-Victorious Love, 422; *TMH*, 278
Love Divine, All Loves Excelling, 384; *TMH*, 283
Make Me a Captive, Lord, 421; *TMH*, 184
More Love to Thee, O Christ, 453; *TMH*, 185
O Come and Dwell in Me, 388; *TMH*, 277
O For a Heart to Praise My God, 417; *TMH*, 282
O For a Thousand Tongues to Sing, 57; *TMH*, 1
O God of Every Nation, 435
O Master, Let Me Walk with Thee, 430; *TMH*, 170
O Thou Who Camest from Above, 501; *TMH*, 172
Prayer for a New Heart, 392
Spirit of God, Descend upon My Heart, 500, *TMH*, 138
Spirit of the Living God, 393

# INDEX OF SUBJECTS AND PERSONS